UNDER THE NORTH LIGHT

The Life and Work of
Maud and Miska Petersham

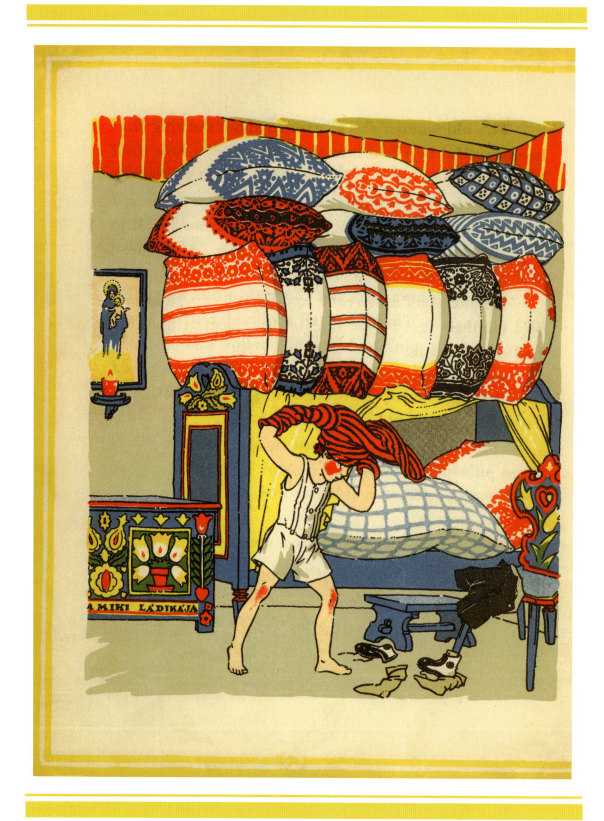

UNDER THE NORTH LIGHT

The Life and Work of
Maud and Miska Petersham

LAWRENCE WEBSTER

FOREWORD BY PHILIP C. STEAD AND ERIN E. STEAD

WOODSTOCKARTS
Woodstock, New York

HALF-TITLE Maud's sketch of a typical work day in the Woodstock studio they built in 1923. Maud and Miska face one another under the north light coming through their large studio window. Son Miki is old enough to join them at his own drawing table. Note the airplane over Maud's head.

FRONTISPIECE Full-page illustration from *Miki*, by Maud and Miska Petersham.

Miska was a perfectionist and real craftsman. He loved to put color in his work and had a strong Magyar feeling for design. The gay painted peasant furniture and the bright colorful embroideries he had known as a boy influenced his pictures. — Maud, 1960

TITLE PAGE Maud and Miska together, circa 1917, the year of their marriage.

ABOVE Illustration from *The Poppy Seed Cakes*. Dog—one of several motifs in the book.

Related title available from WoodstockArts:
Woodstock History and Hearsay (second "art book" edition), by Anita M. Smith

Support for this publication was provided by Shirley Handel.

WOODSTOCKARTS
P.O. Box 1342 Woodstock, NY 12498
T: 845-679-8111 F: 419-793-3452
info@WoodstockArts.com www.WoodstockArts.com

Cataloging-in-Publication Data
Under the North light : the life and work of Maud and Miska Petersham / Lawrence Webster.
Woodstock, NY : WoodstockArts, 2012.
192 p. : ill. ; cm.
Includes bibliographical references and index.
1. Illustrators – United States – Biography. 2. Petersham, Maud Fuller, 1889-1971. 3. Petersham, Miska, 1888-1960.

741.642   NC975.5
                                                                                 .P4
                                                                                 .W43

LCCN: 2012938574
ISBN 13:978-0-9679268-6-5

Book design by Abigail Sturges
Printed in China

CONTENTS

FOREWORD

INTERVIEWER *Has either one of you ever written or illustrated a book without the help of the other?*
MAUD AND MISKA [in unison] *We couldn't do that.*

It's not an easy thing—to draw a rhinoceros. A rhinoceros is a mishmash of unlikely shapes and folds. Get it just a little bit wrong and you end up with an awkward, make-believe dinosaur or some kind of Cubist cow. That's what we say to people who wonder about our collaborative process.

Erin is an outstanding draftsperson. She discovered, though, early in the making of *A Sick Day for Amos McGee*, just how difficult it is to draw a rhinoceros. The weirdness of the animal's form fought against her natural skills. She drew. And erased. And drew. And erased. Frustrated, she went to Phil for help.

"Oh," said Phil, "I've drawn a rhinoceros before! This is how you do it." He grabbed a pencil and quickly doodled a simple rhinoceros onto a scrap of paper. That doodle became Erin's guide for the rhinoceros-who-always-had-a-runny-nose in *Amos McGee*.

That's one example from hundreds of small moments—the natural back and forth of a shared studio. Many of those moments are brief and soon forgotten. Some are brief but bring about sweeping change to a project. In *Amos McGee*, there's a six-page sequence in which the animals leave the zoo, wait for the number five bus, then board the bus en route to Amos's house. As Erin's art developed for this sequence, it became clear to Phil that his own writing was getting in the way.

They talked it over and trimmed six pages of text down to three words: *Later that day . . .*

We are each other's first and most important critic. We react to each other's work in real time, a luxury most authors and illustrators do not have. We save one another from bad ideas, and we help each other recognize good ideas when they come. As you read *Under the North Light*, you will find that Maud and Miska credit one another with the same kind of mutual critique and encouragement.

There are a remarkable number of married couples in the world of children's literature, both in its present and in its past. The Dillons. The Provensens. The Lewins. The D'Aulaires. The Hurds. The Petershams. We suspect this is, in part, because the making of a picture book is such a difficult task. It's not a task to be taken lightly. And not one we would recommend trying alone. This tale of Maud and Miska Petersham's life together sheds light on the powerful and complicated art of intimate collaboration.

We are young, and (with luck) have many more books to come. We can say with certainty, though, that we will never make a book without the help of the other.

Quite simply, to quote the Petershams—we couldn't do that.

– PHILIP C. STEAD AND ERIN E. STEAD
author and illustrator of *A Sick Day for Amos McGee*,
winner of the 2011 Caldecott Medal

Picture from *Get-A-Way and Háry János*, written and illustrated by Maud and Miska Petersham. Below is a note from John Striebel, an artist, creator of the *Dixie Dugan* cartoon strip and a Woodstock neighbor of the Petershams. In the note, which is handwritten, he refers to his two young sons fighting over their new book.

Dear Maudie and Miska,
*   Books arrived OK. Thanks! I think Get-A-Way is simply beautiful and I do hope you do well with it. My little fellow wants it all for his own and the big chap wants it too. Think they will have to be satisfied with half time.*

PROLOGUE

Different Journeys, Same Destination

Every year, thousands of young people arrive in New York City. Many come to seek their fortune and their fame, to earn the confidence born of success in one of the most competitive cities on earth. Many come to escape intolerable conditions at home. And many come for both of those reasons. Today, they come from all over the nation and all over the world: from Indiana and Kansas and California and Texas, from Latin America and Europe and Asia.

It was the same in 1912 as it is today. This tale is about just two of these talented and innovative young people and the artful life they built together over the five decades that would follow.

Maud Fuller, twenty-three, brand-new Vassar degree in hand, arrived in New York City in the summer of 1912. She left her father's Upstate parsonage to attend the New York School of Fine and Applied Art, which had been founded fifteen years earlier by the painter William Merritt Chase. It had not been easy to convince her Baptist parents to let a young, single woman take such an independent step, but Maud prevailed. She moved into a new residence for women art students, the Three Arts Club on West Eighty-fifth Street, and began a year of study at the school, which today is the renowned Parsons school.

Michael Petersham, almost twenty-four, his name anglicized from the Hungarian Petrezse-lyem Mihály, arrived at Ellis Island on September 5, 1912, after seven days in steerage aboard the *Olympic*, a White Star sister ship of the *Titanic*. He brought with him a degree from the rigorous Royal National School for Applied Arts in Budapest, no money, limited English, boundless energy, and an expectation of cowboys and Indians in the streets. He was enthusiastically welcomed by the official on duty. "You're just the kind of young man we need in America," he was told.[1]

It is a remarkable twist of fate—and a stroke of luck for generations of American children—that two people from such disparate backgrounds, arriving in New York from opposite directions, should ever meet. But meet they did, in the drafting room of the International Art Service (IAS), a commercial design studio on West Forty-second Street, opposite the New York Public Library. Founded in 1912 by Arthur F. Wiener and a few other German and Austrian artists steeped in the Art Nouveau energy of Europe, the IAS became one of the first American studios to apply modern sensibilities and techniques to commercial art.

Although Wiener is not a major character in this story, he played a crucial role at the beginning: He had the good sense to hire Michael Petersham in 1913 and, a few months later, to hire the young Maud Fuller. The drafting room at this forward-thinking studio provided an envi-

An early picture of Maud and Miska in their Woodstock studio, bathed in reflected light from the north-facing window. A north light is preferred by many artists for the control it gives them over values, contrasts and subtle color changes in their work.

ronment for the two young artists to hone their craft, to breathe in the fresh energy of a new approach to art. But most important, this studio was the place where they began a courtship—and where they began to work together, setting the course for their entire lives. They would become Maud and Miska Petersham—imaginative, expert artists and warm, iconic figures in a golden age of American children's publishing.

The separate journeys of Maud Fuller and Miska Petersham up to the time of their marriage could not have been more different. And the partnership they built over the next forty years could not have been more rewarding.

CHAPTER 1

Artful Lives

Maud: Independent Yankee

Maud Sylvia Fuller was born in Kingston, New York, on August 6, 1889, the third of four daughters of the Reverend Andrew King Fuller and Phoebe Sisson Fuller. According to Maud's aunt, the Reverend Fuller had been hoping for a son, and on hearing news of a third daughter said, "Throw her out the window!" Late in her life, Maud wrote in a matter-of-fact tone, "I was a great disappointment to my father . . . father was a Baptist minister and with each child he prayed for a boy . . . I was the third girl."[1] Maud was rather cheerful about it, and the fictionalized account in the Petershams' 1932 book *Auntie and Celia Jane and Miki* has a particularly positive interpretation:

> Father loved all his little girls, but he wanted a son very much, so, just in fun, he said, "Throw the new baby out of the window."
>
> The baby's Auntie heard him and she spoke up quickly: "No! No! Give the baby to me."
>
> That baby grew up into a lucky little girl, for she had a Mother and a Father and also Auntie.

Roots

Whatever her father's real feelings about not having a son, the truth is that Maud came from a family that encouraged its women to learn and work just as men did, and to make independent choices in their lives. Maud's granddaughter aptly described the Fullers as "a family of many strong and beautiful women."[2] Maud's mother and her aunt (Auntie, truly like a second mother) lived lives that demonstrated how much they valued hard work, spiritual practice, learning, and loyalty to family and community. These values went back to the Sissons' colonial Puritan, Baptist and Quaker forbears. Much has been written about the American Protestant work ethic, less about how the Quakers have honored the equality of women since their founding in seventeenth-century England.[3] Beyond such culturally inculcated values, the exigencies of daily life in rural Upstate New York required everyone in the family to develop many competencies and to become self-reliant.

Maud's maternal grandfather, Alexander, was one of thirteen children of the sea captain Pardon Sisson and his wife, Mary Slocum. He left Rhode Island as a very young man to join

Brother and sister, Pardon Eugene and Celia Jane
Sisson, Maud's uncle and aunt. Pardon (later "Eugene")
became a math professor at Colgate. Celia Jane, an
elementary schoolteacher, would later be known simply
as "Auntie"; she was a central figure in Maud's life.

his brother Matthew, who had a sheep farm on Muller Hill in Georgetown, New York.[4] Alexander Sisson married Abigail Atwood, with whom he had two children. After her untimely death, he married Abigail Brown, with whom he had three more children, and one of these was Maud's mother, Phoebe.

The Sissons placed enormous value on education for all of their children. The eldest child, Maud's uncle Eugene, became a mathematics professor at Colgate University. Celia Jane, later Maud's beloved "Auntie," was a lifelong teacher. Phoebe was in the 1874 graduating class of Mount Holyoke at a time when only a handful of women went to college.

Life at Holyoke was demanding, requiring rigorous spiritual as well as intellectual and physical discipline. Students were expected to attend church services and prayer meetings and to join Bible study groups. Every dormitory room had two large, lighted closets to give roommates privacy during required daily devotions.[5] Phoebe went directly from Holyoke to New York City to study to be a missionary, hoping to travel the country and the world.

Phoebe's older sister, Celia Jane, appears not to have noticed that women in late-nineteenth-century America had few choices—they had no vote, very few went to college and their status was dependent on that of their husbands or fathers. Auntie's unpublished autobiography, written in 1941 when she was ninety-five, provides insight into the mind and heart of a remarkable woman. Looking back at her long life, she expresses great satisfaction with her teaching career and writes poignantly of her decision never to marry, despite having a long-time ardent suitor:

The contact with school and church had to be met with a very different attitude than that of the factory and farm. . . . I was intensely interested in my new ventures and loved them all . . . I made up my mind not to marry, but to go on with the new work I had chosen. . . . From that day of decision to this I have never had a regret of the step taken and choice made. Here my real life work began, all my energies, zeal and enthusiasm went into the work of church, school and the community around me.[6]

But the younger Phoebe *did* marry—three years after graduation. Andrew King Fuller was from a farm family in Masonville, New York, about thirty miles from the Sisson home. He was a promising young man who had been courting Phoebe Sisson for several years. While Phoebe's ancestors were Rhode Island Quakers, many of them whaling men, Fuller came from Puritan Massachusetts stock—he was a direct descendant of Samuel Fuller, the *Mayflower* ship's doctor. A branch of the Fullers moved to the rolling hills of Delaware County, New York, early in the nineteenth century, and Maud's father was born in 1855, the fourth and youngest child of Sylvia King and Wilder Fuller.

The Fullers valued education as much as the Sissons did. Andrew attended Afton Academy and went on to graduate (in 1879) fourth in his class at Colgate, where he taught elocution for two years after graduating. He attended Hamilton Theological Seminary (now the Colgate-Rochester-Crozer Divinity School), earning a Doctor of Divinity degree in 1882.

Andrew Fuller and Phoebe Sisson married the day he graduated from the seminary. Just three days after that he delivered the graduation address at Afton. "A Youth's Conversation With Himself" still exists in manuscript—thirty-two pages of Fuller's large, confident handwriting. It

Andrew King Fuller, Maud's father, circa 1910. A descendant of the ship's doctor on the *Mayflower*, Fuller grew up on a farm in western New York State. He attended Colgate and received his Doctor of Divinity degree in 1882, two days before marrying Mount Holyoke graduate Phoebe Sisson, Maud's mother.

is clearly the work of a serious and thoughtful young man well read and well schooled in rhetoric. Addressing boys from the same rural region whence he had come, he elaborates on the value of interior dialogue:

> . . . not only do we talk with others—we talk with ourselves. And the most fruitful of all conversations are those that take place when we are withdrawn from the world, have entered into the private apartment of the soul, have turned the key and are alone. Here are made those life choices on which destiny turns. Here are answered those great questions which every soul must answer for itself.

The speech continues in this vein. No listener would have been surprised to learn that Dr. Fuller was headed to the pulpit. But one line, at least, reminds us that he is a bridegroom of just three days. In introducing the topic of conversation, he invokes the heart, rather than the head: "Two Hearts, you know, don't quite understand each other until the contents of one is poured into the listening ear of the other."[7]

Phoebe and Andrew left for Kingston, New York, in September 1882, called by the Wurts Street Baptist Church in the Rondout. Over the next forty years the Fullers would move from there to congregations in Sioux Falls, South Dakota; Newburgh, New York; Scranton, Pennsylvania; and back to the Rondout. Their first three daughters, Ada, Paula and Maud, were born in Kingston, the youngest, Winifred, in Sioux Falls.

Childhood and Youth

Growing up in a parsonage was exacting, but it had its rewards. Fuller was a charismatic and successful churchman. A contemporary in South Dakota observed that he was "a model pastor; his kind, genial manners, his culture and ability, his admirable qualities as a preacher, together with his rare good sense as

Wurts Street Baptist Church in the Rondout district of Kingston was Reverend Fuller's first congregation. Maud and her two older sisters were born here. Fuller later served congregations in Sioux Falls, South Dakota; Newburgh, New York; and Scranton, Pennsylvania. He ended his career back at Wurts Street.

a citizen, secured for him while in Sioux Falls a large circle of friends who greatly regretted his departure."[8] The demands placed on his wife and children were considerable. The four starched and pressed little girls were expected to behave well in church and to comport themselves appropriately at all times.

Religious practice in the family went beyond public observances in church and at prayer meetings. Fuller published seven "Rules of Living" while at Wurts Street, outlining the importance of spiritual practice at a very private level, in a way similar to Phoebe's at Mount Holyoke. The first two of his seven rules were "Never neglect daily private prayer" and "Never neglect daily private Bible reading. . . . All backsliding begins with neglect of these two rules."

For all of this emphasis on private spirituality and public good behavior, however, the Fuller household was far from somber. "A parsonage with four lively girls was certainly not a dull place," said Maud. "One of the many clergymen who visited our home once said that the only way to sleep in our house was to put a pillow over one's head as well as under!" And at the parsonage Maud heard firsthand accounts of life in faraway places by the world-traveling missionaries who were frequent visitors: "The stories told by visiting missionaries at our table were as exciting as fairy tales to me." The house was full of books and conversation and activities. "I loved picture books as a child and was always happy with pencil and paper in my hands," wrote Maud.[9]

Phoebe exerted her influence as well. She chafed a bit at the routines of life as pastor's wife and social leader, perhaps disappointed not to be off on the missionary adventures she had prepared for at Holyoke and the Mission School.[10]

The four Fuller girls. Clockwise from top: Paula, Maud, Winifred and Ada. The sisters would remain close throughout their lives.

My sisters and I fidgeted about through long church services and daily morning prayers, but the stories told by visiting missionaries at our table were as exciting as fairy tales. – Maud

She certainly encouraged her daughters to be independent and to take joy in learning. She raised quite modern women, each ahead of her time. Three of the four girls married, but all had self-supporting careers—unusual in the early twentieth century, even among the educated classes.

Every summer the family returned to Hamilton, New York. "We spent beautiful summer months with our Quaker grandfather."[11] It was here that Auntie kept the promise she had made at Maud's birth: "No! No! Give the baby to me." Maud came to spend six years, summer and winter, with Auntie and her grandfather Sisson in Hamilton. In the Petershams' 1932 book *Auntie and Celia Jane and Miki*, the tale is slightly fictionalized, with a character named Celia Jane standing in for Maud:

> One year, at the end of the summer vacation, the time came when they must all go back to the city. The trunks were all packed again, the sisters each took their share of the left-over bundles and marched to the train.
>
> No one missed Celia Jane when she disappeared from the line. . . . All of the sisters were on the train, all but Celia Jane.
>
> In the hay, 'way up in the top peak of Grandfather's barn, there was a strange hump. At the sound of the whistle of the train, the hump moved, and through the hay up popped Celia Jane's head. She had decided to stay on with Auntie and not go back to the city.

In real life, a year passed between the barn incident and Maud's arrival in Hamilton, the little seven-year-old exclaiming, "Auntie, I have come to live with you and go to your school, Father and Mother said I could!" For Auntie, it was "almost heaven on earth having Maud live with us. She fitted in every crack and crevice and was a very satisfactory child in every respect, anxious to be helpful beyond her years, so affectionate and cheerful . . . six happy years she lived with me, and in the summers the family all came to Hamilton, so there was no long separation."[12] Auntie and Maud both paint a very rosy picture—almost too good to be true— but it does seem certain that theirs was an ideal extended family, one in which individual talents and wishes were honored.

Vassar and New York

When Maud entered Vassar College in Pough-keepsie, New York, in 1908, both of her older sisters had just graduated—Ada in 1906 and Paula in 1907. And during Maud's senior year her younger sister, Winifred, was a freshman. The transcripts for all four Fuller girls show average grades in a liberal arts curriculum. Vassar, along with the other Seven Sisters women's colleges, was a hatchery for women leaders of the early twentieth century—producing leading figures in the arts, business, law, politics, education and publishing. Maud always said that she learned to do research at Vassar—a skill in evidence in many of the Petershams' books, which were often praised for the accuracy and thoroughness of their visual and factual research.

She treasured her Vassar experience and was a loyal alumna, but after the college became co-educational in 1969 the relationship changed. She stopped responding to alumnae appeals[13] and ended up depositing her papers and archives with the de Grummond Children's Literature Collection at the University of Southern Mississippi, an institution with which she had no prior relationship but which was actively and skillfully building its collection throughout the 1960s and 1970s.

Maud was eager to go to art school, so after graduating from Vassar in 1912 she "studied for one easy-going year at the New York School of Fine and Applied Art, living at the Three Arts Club."[14] The Three Arts Club, on West Eighty-fifth Street, was a rather posh residence for single young women studying art in New York City. The New York School of Fine and Applied Art was founded in 1896 by William Merritt Chase.

After her year at art school, Maud traveled from one agency to another looking for work—without success. Arthur Wiener, co-founder of the International Art Service (IAS), held her last hope for employment. When he was on the brink of refusal, Maud burst into tears, and Wiener hired her.[15] He is reported to have said later, "I don't know why I keep you in here; you can't draw a decent line with a pen, pencil, or brush. But you do give a certain moral tone to the office!"[16] It was at IAS that she met a rising young commercial artist named Miska Petersham.

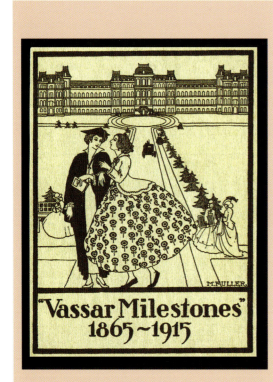

This work signed by Maud Fuller was executed for the Vassar alumnae magazine just three years after she graduated and while she was employed at the International Art Service.

Maud, circa 1914, while working as an artist in New York.

After graduating from Vassar I studied for one year at the New York School of Fine and Applied Art, living at the Three Arts Club. My first job was in the art department of an advertising firm and here I met Miska. — Maud

Miska: Adventurous Magyar

Petrezselyem Mihály was born on September 20, 1888, in Törökszentmiklós, on the northern plains of what was then the powerful Austro-Hungarian Empire. Surname first, a Hungarian language convention, reflected his Magyar heritage. His grandfather was a shepherd on the high plains of Hungary, his father, János, a blacksmith and an official in their small town. When Miska was nine years old the family, including his mother, Fejes Mária, moved to Budapest. He had a tough introduction to the city—classmates laughed at his name, which meant "parsley" in Hungarian.[17]

Along with the obvious differences between Miska's childhood and Maud's, there are striking similarities. Both families encouraged the children in their education and valued independent thinking. Like Maud, Miska spent his childhood summers in the country: "To Miska the happiest days of his childhood were those spent with his grandfather who was a shepherd on the Hungarian plains."[18]

Miska did well in school, and he was an avid reader of adventure stories. The Western novels of the German author Karl May (1842–1912) were a staple. May was a German Zane Grey. He painted a picture of the American West that is mythic and iconic. It is also a picture that is inaccurate, but it intrigued Miska into his adulthood. The young Hungarian was energetic and adventurous, courting trouble by leaping logs and sneaking rides on trolleys across the Danube between Buda and Pest.[19]

Called to Art

"I was born in Hungary on the plains of the Puszta. Having grown up on dry land I always wanted to be a sea captain, so I ended up being an artist,"quipped Miska in a radio interview.[20] In fact, his artistic career began when he was a little boy. When he was six years old, he saved up his pennies for months to buy a small box

Page from a scrapbook that Maud made for her granddaughter, Mary. At the top and at the bottom left are pictures of Miska's family at his father's home in Hungary. The other two photos show Miska as a young man, probably in London or New York in the early 1910s. The handwritten annotations are Maud's.

Miska grew up in a simple Hungarian peasant home with much of the furniture made, carved, and decorated by the father and with brilliant colored embroideries which all Hungarian village women found time to make for their homes. — Maud

of paints that had been beckoning to him from the window of an art supply store. His very first paintings were based on the Hungarian folk designs on his mother's china.[21] Maud would note this affinity for folk design years later: "Miska was a perfectionist and a real craftsman. He loved to put color in his work and had a strong Magyar feeling for design—the gay painted peasant furniture and bright colorful embroideries he had known as a boy influenced his pictures."[22]

Despite their meager resources, Miska's parents sent him to a Real School, similar to an American high school but including two years of community college. His teachers there encouraged him to continue his art studies at the Royal National School for Applied Arts in Budapest. Miska told Maud about his days at art school and she wrote his stories down:

> The comprehensive course of study there introduced him to all kinds of techniques and styles. During the summer months he went to Italy with several other art students and learned to love Venice and Rome where they lived simply with Italian families and painted from morning to night. Then, with the money he made from the pictures he sold upon his return to Budapest, he continued his studies at the Royal Art Academy."[23]

Miska also worked as a tutor/companion to Ernö Balogh, the young son of one of his professors. This relationship bloomed into a deep and familial friendship that would continue for decades. Young Ernö grew up to become a successful concert pianist in the United States and a frequent visitor to the Petersham home in Woodstock, New York. In 1950 he wrote effusively to Maud and Miska:

Watercolor done by Miska while still in art school, showing the image of the traditional shepherd, which he would use over and over, against a background of industrial smokestacks.

. . . how can I tell how happy I was that you heard my concert? I will be grateful to you till my dying day and several years after! Without your financial and moral support I never would dare to come here and never could . . . start to play here. You made my parents also happy and take all the worry away from them, as father always used to say, "as long as Miska is in Amerika I am not worried." . . . The name of "Miska" was a conception in our family representing: ability, reliability, faithfulness, honesty, and talent. Qualities which are eternal, like the Rocks of Gibraltar.[24]

Art school sketch, circa 1908.
Miska's handwritten caption,
a jó pasztor, translates as
"the good shepherd."

*Miska's grandfather was a shepherd
on the plains and from him he learned
to know peasant life.* — Maud

This sketchbook drawing of Miska's
is marked "PAL Grimani s. Polo."
The Palazzo Grimani San Polo,
in Venice, is today a museum.

*During the five years of art school, many
of the students spent summers in Rome
and Venice, living simply and painting
from morning till night.* — Maud, in a
handwritten note about Miska

Page from Miska's
sketchbook while
he was in art school,
circa 1908, with
examples of typical
Hungarian motifs.

*My mother had some
beautiful dishes, so
I painted pictures
of them.* — Miska,
recounting his first
artistic efforts when
he was just six

A page from Miska's
sketchbook. It is after a
Raphael drawing, perhaps
seen in Venice or Flor-
ence. Miska graduated
from art school with high
honors. At the end of
his five years there, the
professors offered him
a three-year scholarship
in a European country
of his choosing, with the
proviso that he agree to
return to Hungary for
the next fifteen years. He
refused, because, as Maud
said, of "his great desire
to travel and know other
countries."

A student sketchbook spread of Miska's, circa 1909. His sense of color was already apparent when he was a student—as was his sense of humor.

Free pass to the Museum of Fine Arts, Budapest, for the academic year 1908–09, issued to Miska when he was in his third year at the Royal National School for Applied Arts.

Promotional flier for the pianist Ernö Balogh (1897–1989), the son of one of Miska's Budapest professors and a lifelong friend. Wishing to support Miska's efforts at getting an education, the elder Balogh hired him as mentor/tutor to young Ernö. Ernö came to the United States in 1924, and enjoyed considerable success. He was friendly with the Hungarian composers Béla Bartók and Zoltán Kodály, arranging Bartók's first U.S. concert tour, in 1927. Ernö remained close to the Petershams, spending weekends and holidays with them in Woodstock. They became estranged after Balogh married Malvina Schweizer, a university professor with left-leaning views.

Budapest to London, London to New York

Miska was just twenty-three when he completed his studies at the Royal National School in 1911. The Balkan war was brewing, and Miska was certain to be drafted into the Austro-Hungarian Army. He was concerned that as a soldier he might sustain injuries to his hands, dashing any hopes of a career in art. Very soon after graduating he booked passage to London, where he had great difficulty finding work. An English friend told him he would never be successful with a name no Englishman was able to pronounce. This friend wrote Miska's name on a piece of paper, crossed out the letters he considered funny and unnecessary, and soon came up with "Petersham." Thus Petrezselyem Mihály became Michael Petersham, known as Miska (pronounced MISH-ka).[25]

Even with the new name he found little opportunity in England. Going days for a time with little or practically no food . . . he was almost ready to give up and bought a revolver from a pawnshop ready to end it all. Sitting in his lodging room after several empty days he heard the postman knock. No one else was in the home and he took the letter handed him, a letter from a young Hungarian friend of his—and enclosed was a gold piece—Miska put away the revolver.[26]

Soon after this he booked steerage passage on the *Olympic*, a White Star sister ship to the *Titanic*. The ship left Southampton on August

Maud's handwritten annotation for a scrapbook, this one describing the challenges faced by Miska during his 1911 sojourn in London.

The months in London were bad. Miska spoke little English. He found but little work for an artist and existed for weeks on end on a one-meal-a-day of fish and chips. With a friend he rented a room on the top floor of this house belonging to a Mrs. Hill. When there was no money for breakfast the boys slept late to make the day shorter. But Mr. Hill (when he felt it was too quiet in their room) would climb the steep, creaky stairs and appear with a tray, a pot of tea, 2 bowls of porridge and the necessary can of sweetened-condensed-milk always with the excuse that his wife had made too much breakfast and didn't want to throw it away.

27, 1912, and arrived in New York a week later. "As the boat approached Ellis Island about which he had heard many strange tales he worried that he would not be accepted, an artist with a very few dollars in his pocket. A doctor examined him, an official questioned him and then patted him on the shoulder, shook his hand and said, 'my boy you are the kind of young man America needs.' And Miska went on his happy way in a new world."[27]

First Years in New York

Miska quickly became acquainted with some fellow Hungarians, including Willy Pogány, a successful book illustrator and set designer. During Miska's first year in New York, Pogány painted a caricature of him, labeling it in large print "Michael 'PETERSHAM,'" perhaps chiding Miska for renouncing his Magyar name, however unpronounceable it was for English speakers. Throughout his life, Miska stayed in touch with several Hungarian immigrants, including Pogány and Ernō Balogh. And he sent boxes of clothes and food to relatives and countrymen.[28]

Miska kept a small notebook, now labeled, in Maud's hand, "Where Miska first looked for a job when he came to New York." Among the forty-seven entries are firms that he believed might be in need of artists—such as publishers and advertising firms. The second to last entry is "International Art Service, Aeolian Hall, 42nd St. opposite Library—this studio German style."[29] Here he found work and met Maud.

Caricature of Miska by Willy Pogány, 1912. Pogány's label, "Michael PETERSHAM," pokes fun at Miska's anglicized name. Many Hungarians came to New York in the first two decades of the twentieth century. Miska became a citizen in 1922, shortly before passage of the U.S. Immigration Act of 1924 and the tight quotas it imposed.

Maud and Miska Petersham: Artful Marriage, Artful Lives

Maud and Miska met in the IAS drafting rooms very soon after the 1913 Armory Exhibition, a seismic event in the New York art world. The Armory Exhibition was an enormous assemblage of over thirteen hundred works by more than three hundred avant-garde European

Willy Pogány, a Hungarian illustrator, artist and set designer, had attained considerable success in New York by the time Miska arrived in 1912. Pogány was a generous friend and mentor.

Miska, center, with two unidentified friends during his early years in New York. Miska enjoyed playing cards throughout his life and was known as a rapacious bridge player, much sought after as a partner in Woodstock.

and American artists. This was the first time most Americans had seen the work of Picasso, Matisse, Gauguin and Duchamp. The press and the public found much of the fauvist and cubist work scandalously radical, and even President Roosevelt declared, "That's not art!"[30]

The IAS was very much a part of this new and cosmopolitan art world in New York. Founded in 1912 by German and Austrian émigré artists, the firm (on Forty-second Street, opposite the New York Public Library) was "one of the first design studios in the U.S. to apply modern ideas to advertising art." Co-founder Arthur Wiener introduced the notion of coherent graphic persona for a corporation—what today we call "branding."[31] He was a frequent speaker on commercial and graphic art, espoused his theories and kept IAS in the public eye.[32] Maud and Miska remained friends with Wiener well after they moved on in their careers. Among the other IAS artists they befriended was Paul T. Frankl, a Viennese immigrant who would become an iconic figure in American modernism. Frankl later visited the Petershams in Woodstock and eventually bought his own small weekend house in nearby Bearsville.

Miska took an interest in Maud's work from the beginning. Years later, after winning the Caldecott Medal, they related to Irene Smith Green the story of a three-year courtship disguised as a mentorship, and Green retold it this way:

> This Petersham offered to look over her drawings and to criticize them professionally. He came early in the mornings and cut short his lunch hours to help Maud Fuller improve her work. Soon he was worrying because Maud was "wasting her time." He persuaded her to go home (then Newburgh) and draw. He would come up weekends to view her progress. Perhaps he did come as an art critic, not suitor; anyhow his displeasure frightened Auntie. Miska explained to her that he could not afford the train fare unless Maud worked seriously! He said she must be free from the interruptions and demands of a large family, and spend a definite number of hours each day at her drawing board. Once understanding the problem, Auntie became Miska's ally for all time. He might have seemed out of place in the Fuller family (for he was a Catholic, a foreigner, and an impecunious artist); but Auntie understood him and loved him. Also, she took over some of Maud's household chores.[33]

With Auntie's help, the Fuller family came to know and appreciate this robust, exotic man. On April 17, 1917, three years after Maud and Miska met, they were married in the living room of the Fuller parsonage, with Maud's father officiating. Auntie's autobiography provides us with a taste of their early married life:

> Miska and Maud rented an apartment in NY, tiny but so homey and livable; a veritable paradise all their own. . . . While on this visit, Miska invited me to live with them, saying, "We want you to stay and be our Auntie forever. Paula has Father and Mother Fuller to live with them and we want you!" And I became a member of the Petersham family . . .[34]

The newlyweds lived in the artistic Greenwich Village district of New York, first on West Eleventh Street and then on Washington Square. Soon Miska's friend Willy Pogány passed on to them some work that he had no time to do. Within months they were working steadily on illustrations for children's magazine pieces, textbooks and trade books. They became known for their ability to meet deadlines, their competence, their hard work and their talent. While still in their twenties, the couple were well on their way to becoming leaders in the field of children's illustration.

These were wartime years, and although America was isolationist at the beginning of the war in Europe, after the sinking of the *Lusitania* in 1915 American attitudes toward Germans grew hostile. The atmosphere must have been difficult for some of the German and Austrian artists at IAS, and disturbing for European artists all over New York. Wiener himself wrote letters to newspapers arguing that the press's demonizing of the German army was one-sided; after the war, in 1919, he was arrested for espionage and interned at Ellis Island.[35] The United States passed its first Selective Service law in

April 1917. Just five months later, Miska, though not yet a citizen, was issued a certificate by the neighborhood draft board exempting him from military service, since he was "a married man with a dependent wife."[36]

Woodstock

In 1920 Maud and Miska started renting a summer home in the artists' colony of Woodstock, nestled in the Catskill Mountains in New York State. Since 1902, when the Englishman Ralph Radcliffe Whitehead and his Philadelphia-born wife, Jane Byrd McCall, founded the Byrdcliffe colony on Mount Guardian above Woodstock, the little town had become host to artists, musicians, actors, sculptors and all manner of writers. A pamphlet published several years after the founding of the colony extols the virtues of Woodstock's cultural and intellectual scene:

> Woodstock . . . is today a nationally known locality, famous for the breadth of its mental and cultural outlook and the diversity of its interests and people. Among its residents . . . there are probably more celebrities, more nationalities, more people of creative ability, than there are to be found in any other section of the country. It is a place where one may work without interruption, enjoy oneself without censure, hold strange opinions without suffering for them, and be judged by what one is and does rather than what one has.
>
> Woodstock is a place of extremes and of paradoxes. . . . not a fashionable place, yet it sets fashions . . . extravagantly informal . . .
>
> It is the most cosmopolitan village in the world . . . People do not come to Woodstock to retire and die; they come here to live![37]

New Baby, New House

In July 1923 Maud returned to the city for the birth of their first and only child. Writing years later, Auntie hints through her joy that this birth was not an altogether easy process:

> After a week of intense anxiety there comes flashing over the wires the good news that Miska and Maud are the parents of a twelve-pound boy, and there is great rejoicing in all our hearts. His

Announcement hand-lettered by Maud and Miska upon the birth of their son, Miska Fuller Petersham (Miki), in New York, 1923.

Greetings from MAUD and MISKA'S little MISKA FULLER PETERSHAM July 13, 1923

Young Miska Fuller Petersham (Miki) with Celia Jane Sisson (Auntie), circa 1925. Auntie moved in with the Petershams shortly after their marriage in 1917. She remained a beloved member of their household, and its stalwart manager, until her death at age ninety-eight in 1944. She took on much of the care and raising of Miki, just as she had done for Maud.

name is Miska Fuller Petersham, called Miki. (And I am supremely happy that my dearest Maud and Miska have placed so much confidence in me trusting their sweet Miki to my care and protection through the years of his childhood.)[38]

They returned to the rented cottage in Woodstock, Maud arriving with babe in arms and saying, "'See Auntie, what I have brought you?' . . . and soon went to the studio with Miska and at their drawing table face to face are soon in deep thought only of the subject before them."[39] The Petershams' niece Mitzi Shewmake, a frequent visitor throughout her childhood, also remembers that when Maud and Miska were working in the studio they were not to be disturbed—unless one was asked to model—but that this was not much of a hardship since there was always the watchful eye of Auntie, who was endlessly imaginative in keeping children happily engaged.

During the busy summer of 1923 Maud and Miska bought land from Ralph Whitehead at

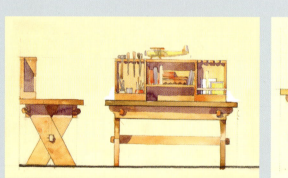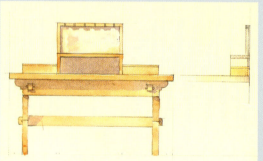

Drawings by Maud and Miska for a line of children's furniture. Maud's handwritten notes suggest that a boy could put his supplies for model airplanes in some of the cubbyholes and that a girl would have space for her paper dolls.

the edge of Byrdcliffe and began to construct a sprawling stone house. The Petersham house differs from other Byrdcliffe structures in that it is made of stone rather than wood, but is very much in the spirit of the place—solid, quirky and clearly handcrafted. Miska stood over the stonemasons, remembering Hungarian peasant buildings, and the house and grounds are full of handmade touches: carvings, stonework and stained glass. He built and painted much of the furniture himself.[40]

In an article published the year after they moved in, Maud explains that they got some of the ideas for their house well before they bought land and started to build:

> We draw houses we think it would be fun to live in . . . You may not agree with us that the house we planned for the Three Bears is much to be preferred to an ordinary domicile, but we think so and have built a home like it under the pines. We like the holes in the shape of hearts that we made in the furniture so we have holes in the shape of hearts in our benches and chair-backs and window shutters. They make wonderful places for our small boy to stick his fingers through.[41]

A 1929 review of a small exhibition of the Petershams' illustrations at the Woodstock Public Library gives a sense of the atmosphere of their house: "They have been able to impress their vision on the builders so well that their house is almost as personal as one of their colored drawings . . ."[42]

Family Life

Theirs was a welcoming and elastic household. In 1926 Maud was invited to write an article for the *Elementary English Review*. She began by explaining who was who in the household:

> First . . . we are not sisters, although one reviewer did speak of "the work of the Petersham girls." Miska is Miska, and I am his wife, and the

The house the Petershams built at the edge of Byrdcliffe, in Woodstock, New York, in 1923–24. Miska built much of the furniture himself. The table to the left of the staircase was later repurposed as a bedstead for one of Maud and Miska's great-grandchildren. Much of the artwork they created themselves, while other pieces they collected during their travels.

Maud and Miska's small print of the herb shop and garden of their friend and neighbor, the artist, herbalist and Woodstock historian Anita Smith.

rest of our family consists of a baby, an Auntie, and a black cat. Auntie supervises the wheels of our domestic machinery, baby indulges in the usual activities characteristic of an almost two-year-old, and the black cat doesn't do a thing except that he occasionally officiates as a model.[43]

This initial family of four—Maud, Miska, Auntie and baby Miki (plus cat)—often expanded to include guests from New York or from Hungary, members of Maud's family and, later, their two grandchildren. Maud and Miska routinely hired new immigrants as domestic help. Maud's three sisters and parents were frequent visitors, and Mary (later "Mitzi" Byrd—daughter of Maud's younger sister, Win-

ifred—spent many long months during the summer with the Petershams. A custom among some forward-thinking families of the time—addressing one's parents by their given names—found its way into the Petersham/Fuller culture. Winifred encouraged her daughter to call her "Wini," and Maud and Miska were "Maudy" and "Miska" to Miki, as they eventually would be to their two grandchildren and to the children of their Woodstock friends.

Members of the Woodstock Community
They were very much an admired part of the Woodstock community. Orville Peets, a local writer said, "I doubt if there are two

more productive artists in Woodstock than Maud and Miska Petersham."[44] A roster of Woodstock artists published in the *Bulletin of the Woodstock Historical Society* in 1930 includes the Petershams among one hundred and thirty-eight artists; twenty of these were part of a married couple, but only the Petershams worked collaboratively.[45] They had a wide circle of creative friends, among them Mabel and Ned Chase, Ruth and Sandor Harmati, Wilna Hervey and Nan Mason, Dorothy and Neil Ives, Vadia and Vladimir Padwa, and Fritzi and John Striebel. Maud kept a food journal, with notes on parties they attended as well as plans for and reports on her own hostessing adventures. A 1938 note about an evening at the home of the musician Vladimir Padwa and his wife, Vadia, captures something of the old Woodstock—its internationalism as well as its sense of fun:

Padwas' Sunday Evening Supper: The long table in kitchen—dish of red caviar at each end of table—bottle of vodka—real black pumpernickel bread—drink vodka "bottoms up." Cold meat loaf and a reddish potato, beets, sour cream dressing salad/delicious! Then a hot consommé as a course after the meat and salad. . . . Then in the other room and music. Piano arrangements (by Liszt) of Schubert's songs. Very beautiful.

She jotted down plans for their own parties, including the following: "A party we want to have—Haggis (scotch oat meal and liver cooked in sheep's stomach—can use greased cloth if nec-

"New Years Eve—1938—Eco and Joli Stallforth's." An entry in "My Food Book," Maud's journal of parties and meals in the years 1938 through 1958. This is the first entry, describing a party given by their Byrdcliffe neighbors Federico Stallforth and his Hungarian wife, Jolanda Papp. Years later, the sprawling Arts and Crafts "cottage" where this gathering took place became the Woodstock residence of the folk singer Bob Dylan. Maud paid close attention to the food and drink on offer at such events, giving us a glimpse into Woodstock's social life. Her note in the bottom-right corner says, "felt fine next day."

essary) . . . Drink with it—Whisky mixed with honey and whipped cream."[46]

The joys of Woodstock were hard to find elsewhere. Maud wrote a homesick note from Texas to their good friends Wilna Hervey and Nan Mason: "Just now it seems lonesome for most of the other people we have met are nice but just regular." Miska added a postscript: "Just to let you know how much . . . we miss you both . . ."[47]

"Joy for Gioja," a get-well message with folk-art flowers and hand-lettering by Miska. Gioja Webster, a Byrdcliffe neighbor and friend, had come down with measles after weeks of nursing her three little girls back to health. Measles was a very dangerous disease in 1940, requiring darkened rooms and weeks of care. This picture and the sentiment behind it must have done much to cheer up the patient.

Community Life

They became prominent citizens as well as prominent artists. Miska was an avid golfer and served on the board of governors of the Woodstock Country Club. He also served on the library board, and they both volunteered their artistic services and lively imaginations in the planning of community events and fund-raisers. Jane Whitehead named Miska in her will as one of a small committee that she hoped would own and manage Byrdcliffe after her family was gone—people who understood the spirit of Byrdcliffe.[48]

One of their community contributions still prances in the Woodstock Public Library. "Become the proud owner of a unique example of an all-but-lost art, a hand-carved, hand-decorated horse, painted and signed by some of Woodstock's most famous artists," went the pitch at the 1954 Woodstock Library Fair, an annual event that decided the library's operating budget for the next year. These merry-go-round horses were carved from oak by the local folk artist William Spanhake, and the "famous artists" who decorated them included the Petershams as well as Edward Chavez, Julio de Diego and Howard Mandel. The horse painted by Miska and Maud resides to this day in the children's room of the Woodstock Library, for the climbing and riding pleasure of anyone who visits. A handful of people in Woodstock today remember firsthand encounters with Maud and Miska—a few neighboring children served as models and played with their grandchildren—and their Glasco Turnpike house is not much changed, looking inviting and a little mysterious. But Peter the Horse is the most-touched symbol of Maud and Miska's involvement in the local community.[49]

Maud between two of her dear friends, Wilna Hervey and Nan Mason, at the Woodstock Valentine's Ball in 1942, a benefit for the Red Cross. Hervey was well known as a silent film actress, playing "The Powerful Katrinka" in the Toonerville Trolley films of the 1920s. Mason, an artist, was Hervey's lifelong companion.

In addition to designing the program for this ball, the Petershams served on committees and boards in Woodstock, supporting the library, the golf club and Byrdcliffe. Miska was active in the Republican Party.

A Christmas card lino block inscribed from Miki (the Hungarian message translates to "Christmas Greetings"). It was common in Woodstock for even non-artists to make their own Christmas cards; often, for the first few Christmases after the birth of a beloved child, that child would be the signer, as here.

Peter the Horse, carved by folk artist William Spanhake and painted by the Petershams, as he appears today in the children's room of the Woodstock Public Library. Countless youngsters have climbed the booster steps for a ride, and many adoring arms have encircled Peter's neck since he moved into the library in the 1950s. Peter was one of five horses carved by Spanhake and painted by different Woodstock artists for an auction to benefit the library.

Working Together: The Art of Collaboration

The Petershams considered themselves a single creative force: Their writing and their illustration were "by Maud and Miska Petersham," with no distinction as to who did what to create the book one holds in one's hands. Creative collaboration, particularly in the context of a marriage, can be intriguing.[50] How did two such different people sustain an artistic collaboration over the span of forty years? It is not possible to draw up a definitive list of guidelines for such a relationship, but there are glimpses and hints in Maud and Miska's comments about their work and in their shared studio.

Process

When asked about the process by which they created books, they often mentioned differences between them, and how these actually strengthened the partnership. An obvious physical difference was that Maud was left-handed and Miska right-handed. "It may seem strange that two people can work on the same book and the same pictures," said Miska. "I have jokingly said that Maud puts in the left eye in a drawing and I the right." But in the same interview he took a deeper look at the nature of their collaboration: "What really happens is that Maud likes to start things and I am strong on the finish." Maud's explanation was similar: "When I want to be funny about it, I say that Miska does the right hand side, because I'm left-handed and he's right-handed. But really, we both work on the drawings—I love to start them and then I get very tired of it and I turn them over to Miska and he loves to finish. . . ."[51]

However lightly they spoke of it, their handedness influenced the way they worked together spatially: opposite one another at large drawing boards, next to the enormous north-facing

The Petershams' house seen from the north, circa 1946. The studio window is in the wing on the right.

A sketch by Maud of herself and Miska hard at work on Lemon Island in the St. Lawrence River near Gananoque, Ontario.

window. The light entered on Maud's right, Miska's left, ergonomically just so—no shadows. Their studio, in the self-contained west wing of the house, was a large room with high ceilings and a cheerful fireplace, plenty of books and references, toys, and souvenirs from all over the world. They kept a rigid schedule, isolating themselves deliberately from the busy world in the rest of the house.

Their shared pleasure in their work held them together as well. "Working together on books for children was our joy as well as our work. Fortunately we complemented each other. Miska was a perfectionist and I loved the planning of a book and ideas came easily to me. . . . We both had the hope that our books would not only give pleasure to a child but be meaningful and worthwhile."[52] They strove to keep their young readers deeply engaged.

Throughout the complicated process that brought a book from idea to dummy to finished product, ready to go to press, they maintained a spirit of goodwill and respect for one another. A sense of humor helped. In one interview Miska poked fun at himself and his sometimes overbearing personality: "Mrs. Petersham does all the work. I do all the criticizing."

INTERVIEWER: Has either one of you ever written or illustrated a book without the help of the other?
MAUD AND MISKA [in unison]: We couldn't do that.[53]

Maud had good advice for aspiring writers and illustrators. She spoke about "building a book." She used dummies, doing the illustrations first and then filling in the text—often, if stuck, starting in the middle. She also said that one cannot always count on getting inspiration out of the blue, but that if you diligently go to the studio and sit at the drawing board, then you are creating space for ideas to emerge.[54]

While their studio was a creative haven, they also traveled—both for inspiration and for a change of scene in which to work. For several summers they went to Gananoque, Ontario, near the Thousand Islands in the St. Lawrence River. "We did some of our finest work there,"

Christmas 1927:
The Magi, with folk
elements visible in
their costume and
in the border of
the card.

wrote Maud.[55] And in the late 1940s they kept a pied-à-terre on Bank Street in New York City.

Often, research was the primary purpose of their travels. They went to Holland and Palestine, Sarasota and Williamsburg to gather material for books set in those places. They made copious sketches while traveling, to use as references when back home in the studio.

As a minister's child, Maud was steeped in the Bible, and she brought this experience to her visual appreciation of Palestine. There, "all the Bible stories I learned as a child became a truth . . . when we stood in the market place in Jerusalem, the Bible figures were right there in front of us just as they might have been 2000 years ago. The camels, and the shepherds with their long eared sheep passed like a parade in front of us."[56]

Partnerships in Printing and Publishing

Maud and Miska collaborated effectively not only with one another, but also with their editors and their printers. They began their work at a most exciting time in children's book publishing, working closely with the legendary May Massee at Doubleday and then at Viking. Massee was known for discovering and encouraging artists and writers—she published the first four of the Petershams' original works, as well as many books that they illustrated. Maud credited her with not only giving them a wonderful start, but also keeping them on a rewarding, creative, productive path. She describes their first meeting:

Just at that time we were a bit downhearted as one publisher had suggested that we could illustrate for him "The Wind in the Willows" but the next day he sent a polite note telling us that he could not give us the contract as he had just discovered Miska was an enemy alien (at that time Miska only had his first citizenship papers of which he was very proud).

It was in May's office that the stars came out for us—she became our publisher and close friend. As editor she had the imagination and the vision to see the possibilities in a rough dummy or even in a half-formed idea for a book. Her judgment was quickly given and if she approved it was because of her enthusiasm and encouragement that the book became a reality.[57]

Doris Patee, Maud and Miska's Macmillan editor for much of their mid-career and later work, including their Caldecott books, became a close friend as well as a colleague. She helped them to find their Bank Street apartment and welcomed them into her busy New York circle.

Maud and Miska's contribution to the printing processes that were so rapidly developing in the 1920s and 1930s cannot be overstated. "An illustration could be defined as a picture that can be printed," the illustrator Ed Emberley has said. "A good picture is a bad illustration if it cannot be printed well."[58] Acutely aware of this, Miska in particular spent endless hours with his printers, helping to develop new techniques and ensuring the highest possible standards. Beatrix Potter is said to have done the same alongside Frederick Warne in turn-of-the-century London. She was often described as heavily involved in the production process, just as the Petershams were, as related by Maud herself: "In fact we are really fussy and at times I fear a little troublesome to our publishers."[59]

They worked particularly closely with two printers who turn up in all of the history books that recount events in children's publishing in the United States, Charles Stringer and William Glaser. Stringer perfected a process that enabled cost-effective full-color printing, a process that was used by many of the important children's publishers of the time, including May Massee's Doubleday. William Glaser, along with this wife, Lillian, developed a process for full-color printing in offset lithography. Miska painstakingly helped to work out the details of this "Glaser process," making separations on zinc or glass plates, something that required great precision and endless patience. He was helped by Sam Wiley, a Woodstock artist hired by Maud and Miska to assist with this difficult process. Wiley worked with the Petershams for years, even traveling with them to Canada on one occasion. Bill and Lillian Glaser became much more than colleagues—they became fast friends of the Petershams. Their attention to detail as well as the relationship between the couples is clear in a note from Miska in Woodstock to Maud in New York, seeing the Glasers about a book (probably *America's Stamps*): "Maudy dear . . . please ask Bill and Lillian to have the outline on the mountain removed from the halftone plate, as we forgot to mark it in red for guide line only. I am sorry for the trouble it will entail, but it is easily done I think. . . . Please give my love to Bill and Lillian."[60]

Complementary Temperaments, Shared Values, Mutual Respect

While Maud and Miska had quite different personalities—Miska was a big presence, hearty and humorous; Maud was soft-spoken and was known to fall asleep when a party went late or when the political opinions got loudly expressed—they shared many values.

They had a common interest in health and well-being. Miska believed in cold showers—he installed an outdoor shower—and exercise. He also had a daily habit that, he claimed, was responsible for his good eyesight throughout his entire life: He would immerse his face in a basin of cold water and bathe his eyes by rolling them around. Maud, as evidenced by her food journals, was keenly interested in food and its effects, and they both worked in their vegetable garden. Together they embarked on self-improvement adventures, including a 1945 visit to the legendary Kellogg spa in Battle Creek, Michigan. From Battle Creek they wrote to the Glasers of salt baths and massages, and the trials of not smoking. They both smoked cigarettes—and tried to break the habit more than once. In an anecdote related by the family, Maud and Miska told each other that they had quit but kept cigarettes at opposite ends of the house, entreating family members and visitors not to tell the other about their transgressions.[61]

Maud kept her religious faith throughout her life, although she was not a churchgoer as an adult. In 1959 she commiserated about the death of a beloved friend: "How sad are so many of the things that one must face. Only a trust in a divine purpose makes it possible . . ."[62] Miska was raised a Catholic but did not practice or claim any particular faith. He did, however, believe in the supernatural. He was a spiritualist and served as a medium at séances held at their home. Miska once told young Miki not to be afraid of ghosts: They will be friendly if you talk with them politely, he explained. When Miska's stepmother died in Hungary, Maud felt cold and they both sensed her in the room.[63] And when Miki was serving in the Pacific during World

War II, Miska assured Maud confidently that their son was alive and well.[64]

They appreciated nature and had a sense of environmental issues that were not yet being generally articulated. In a note addressed "to the children of Haddonfield," Maud describes a particular moment when nature inspired reverence and awe in the couple:

Miska and I went on a long trip in Canada, and we drove through forests with trees so high and so close together that there seemed to be no sky. . . . Then we drove past the mills and all about were immense piles of logs higher and larger than the buildings of the mill. All these trees were being turned into paper.

It made us feel very solemn and serious. The great trees would become paper. Then the pictures we made would be printed on that white paper. We decided we better be very careful and make pictures good enough to make up for the cutting down of those trees.[65]

Their abiding attachment to one another appears from time to time in remnants of notes and stories. Miska once wrote when Maud was away for a few days, "I am kind of lost without you and I do not know what to do about it. . . . I want to talk to you even though I have nothing particular to say." In what is perhaps a telling sign of the breadth of their relationship, this very loving note ends with a reference to their work: "you have a very nice letter here from Miss Patee [their editor]. She is still afraid of the brown being too dark. So when you see all the proofs . . . we will have to decide on the lighter brown."[66]

At times Miska considered himself a "mere" illustrator—less than the painter he had wanted to be when he was a young art student. The distinction between "fine art" and "illustration" was elusive, and many in the field of illustration defended themselves against the view that their art was somehow less than fine. "What journalism is to literature, illustration is to art, the illustrator Robert Weaver once argued, " . . . the illustrator may use the ideas of the contemporary painter, but it is communication that is his ultimate goal."[67] Albert Dorne was more defensive: "in translating the requirements of an advertising director or magazine art editor into a picture, there is no reason why the same standards of art cannot as appropriately be applied here as for gallery walls."[68]

Honors and Recognition

The Petershams were genuinely humble, neither falsely modest about their work nor grandiose about their legacy and the many honors that came their way. Maud, in a handwritten draft for Miska's obituary, said simply, "He married an American girl who was also an artist and from then they worked together writing and illustrating children's books and set a higher standard for the books for children then being published."[69]

Even at the beginning of their career, the Petershams' work was singled out. The American Institute of Graphic Arts recognized four of their books in three highly competitive exhibitions on the best of American Book Illustration. In 1926 *Nursery Friends From France* was one of just sixty-five books chosen from a field of two hundred and sixty. The 1927 show included two Petersham books, *Children of the Mountain Eagle* and *Tales Told in Holland*, among its two hundred and sixty. Perhaps most rewarding of all, *Get-A-Way and Háry János*, which the Petershams wrote as well as illustrated, was one of a mere seventeen books selected from a field of two hundred and sixty. *Get-A-Way* was in good com-

pany: Other artists with work represented in the New York show included Peggy Bacon, Wanda Gag, José Clemente Orozco, Edward Steichen, and Lynd Ward.[70]

Their highest honors were the 1946 Caldecott Medal for *The Rooster Crows* and the 1942 Caldecott Honor status for *An American ABC*. These Caldecott awards, bestowed by the American Library Association since 1938, not only ensure that the featured work will stay in print indefinitely but also excite interest in an artist's other work.

Miska quite realistically said they appreciated the medal because it spurred the sale of their other books.[71] Louise Seaman Bechtel, writing to congratulate Maud and Miska on this honor, downplays the value of the award itself: "Medals are fun because they give a lot of people, including me, a special chance to say thank you."[72] After receiving the Caldecott Medal, the Petershams were invited to endorse artists' products, including Grumbacher watercolors in an advertisement appearing in the October 1948 issue of *Art Digest*. The copywriter puffed a bit: "The strength and vigor of their illustrations are easily traceable to their successful collaboration which contributes to the rare charm that makes their works collector items."[73]

Later Years

Miki enlisted in the service and trained for the Army Air Corps at Fort Edwards, California. When one of his close friends at Fort Edwards, Ted Reagan, got married, his sister, Marj Reagan, from Girard, Ohio, went out for the wedding. Marj hit it off with Miki, and they married six months later—on January 25, 1943, just before both Ted and Miki were sent off to serve on the Pacific front.

Maud and Miska would not meet their new daughter-in-law until after the war. Maud wrote about the newlyweds to a friend in 1945: "Now if only the time comes when these boys are safe and sound, won't that be the happiest day of all our lives? . . . Marj (her name is Marjory Ann Reagan but they call her Marj) writes us very sweet happy letters and we shall just keep our fingers crossed."[74] After the war, Miki, who now called himself Mish, moved to New Jersey with his wife and new daughter, Mary, born in 1946. Next they settled in Cleveland, where a second child, Michael, was born in 1950 while Mish was studying at the Cleveland Art Institute. Soon the young family moved to Fort Lauderdale, Florida, and founded a pottery, the House of Petersham. This was a short-lived endeavor, and when Mish was offered a faculty position at Kent State University they moved permanently to Ohio. Following family tradition, they spent every summer in Woodstock, and the children developed lifelong friendships there.

Miska had a close and whimsical relationship with his grandchildren. Over Maud and Miska's bed were two ceramic angels, "Angel Looking Up" and "Angel Looking Down," part of a crèche they had made when Mary was very young. Mary remembers the angels well, having always been drawn to them when she visited. Miska, missing Mary in far-off Ohio, sent her a note, enclosing the angels and describing a bit of unexplainable magic:

> Mary darling, This morning Maud and I looked up at the window and there were the most beautiful white mountains and forests you have ever seen, then a movement in the middle of it as if a little animal started moving in the trees and suddenly there was a little movement in our bed and a little gentle voice said, "Maudy, can I have the angel?" So Maudy reached for Angel Looking

Miki, now known as "Mish," in an airplane. He joined the Army Air Corps during World War II and served from August 8, 1942, to January 14, 1946.

The Petershams created many original Christmas cards. In this one from the World War II era, the angel looking at our world is profoundly sad.

This earlier card—dated 1937—shows a bewildered angel, holding a small green branch, amidst Manhattan traffic.

From 1932: Will Santa sleep through his job? The reindeer peering through the window do look worried!

Crèche made for the Petersham grandchildren, early
1950s. Maud created the
ceramic figures, Miska the
painted box. Nowadays their
great-grandchildren enjoy the
crèche every Christmas.

Maud and Miska at work
in the ceramics studio
on the figures for their
Christmas crèche.

Down, then for Angel Looking Up. . . . But when she turned around to give the angels, there was no Mary in our bed, but there was the most beautiful sun ray on the spot where Mary should have been sitting and the sunbeam came through the window where the white mountains and trees were, only now was a big clear hole where evidently little Mary walked through to come in our bed and then before we could catch her she ran back and through the forest to her own big bed in Cleveland, so Maudy and Miska only had the sun ray to keep them company.[75]

The Petershams collaborated closely on gifts for their grandchildren. One of Maud's hobbies was ceramics, and Miska enjoyed building furniture and other woodworking projects. Maud referred to these endeavors as their form of play, which brought them together to create one-of-a-kind gifts for their grandchildren. It is easy to imagine the autumn evenings leading up to Christmas, with Maud and Miska putting their heads together to design and build a crèche or a replica of Noah's Ark. The crèche, which their granddaughter still takes out every Christmas for her own children and grandchildren, is populated with ceramic figures by Maud in a painted wooden stable built by Miska. The colorful ark was built and painted by Miska and peopled with figures of Noah, Mrs. Noah, and many animal pairs, all sewn and stuffed by Maud.

Maud Alone

During the 1950s Miska and Maud traveled to Florida in the winters, often staying at Longboat Key, near Sarasota, and in a small house they bought in Fort Lauderdale. Maud's sister Winifred lived in Arlington, Virginia, where she was the executive secretary at St. Agnes School.

The Petershams were staying with her in the winter of 1959–60 when Miska fell ill and was admitted to the hospital, to be diagnosed with a rare form of liver cancer. He died three months later.

A few days before Miska's death, Maud wrote a note to their editor, Doris Patee, from his bedside:

Page from "The Brown Elf of the Cypress Tree and Jerry," an unpublished manuscript created by Maud in the mid-1960s, after Miska's death. It is the story of a boy in Florida whose father works at Cypress Gardens and believes in Little People, such as elves. Note Maud's handwritten critique to the boy's right, under the pictures on the wall: "should be younger." This is one of several unpublished projects that Maud worked on during the 1960s.

Dear Doris,

They don't feel that Miska can last through the day—he has the most powerful will to live which the doctors cannot understand at this point. If only he can go today—I can't take it much longer. . . .

[p.s.] It is now very early Monday morning—yesterday Miska rallied—ate his meals and talked with us—he is so sweet but determined not to give up. He sleeps much of the time. Don't know what today will bring.[76]

THE WHITE HOUSE
WASHINGTON

August 1, 1968

Dear Mrs. Petersham:

Collecting children's books is a very special hobby of mine, and I am fortuante to have many of the books which you and your husband have so beautifully illustrated.

Do you think that if I sent my copies to you, you could autograph them for me? If this would be possible, please let me know where to send them. I can't tell you how much this would mean!

With best wishes,

Sincerely,

Lynda J Robb

Lynda Johnson Robb

Mrs. Maud Petersham
c/o The Macmillan Company
866 Third Avenue
New York, New York 10022

Fan mail from the White House, 1968. President Johnson's elder daughter, Lynda Johnson Robb, asked Maud to autograph her copies of their books.

Maud wrote soon afterward that Miska might have had a premonition of his death:

That last month before Miska went to the hospital, he said something that at the time I couldn't understand. Now I realize he already sensed what was ahead. We had gone for a short walk. Cars passed, we heard a plane overhead, birds were chirping and a dog barking, in one of the apartments a child was crying. Miska stopped walking and listened then said, "Isn't it strange, the world goes on just the same."[77]

Maud returned to Woodstock and invited her older sister, Ada, a retired Latin teacher, to leave the retirement home where she resided and move in with her. She arranged for Miska's burial in a family plot in Hamilton, New York. Obituaries in the *New York Times* and the *Washington Post* outlined the facts of Miska's life, but Patee, their long-time editor at Macmillan, captured the spirit of the man: "Miska was a wonderful person, and you have had many good years together. . . . how many times he talked of his early years, and he was a marvelous storyteller."[78]

Maud soon set to work on *The Shepherd Psalm*, an illustrated version of the Twenty-third Psalm, "The Lord Is My Shepherd." Maud's explication and illustrations are erudite and bring out the comforting nature of this much-used text. The book was published just two years after Miska died, and it is an inspirational example of the alchemy of turning mourning into creative work.

In 1962 Maud sold the big house and studio and, with Ada, moved nearer to the village, into a smaller dwelling. She had never learned to drive, and Miska had been in charge of the practical side of their household. Old friends and neighbors characterized this new house as "utterly

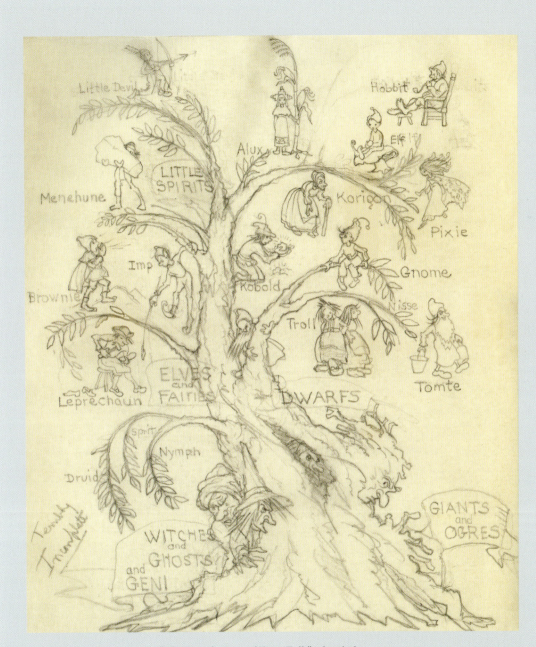

"The Family Tree of Fairy Folk": sketch for
"Who's Who in Fairylore," a book planned by Maud.

Maud and her older sister, Ada Fuller, in 1957. Ada, the eldest of the four Fuller sisters, taught high-school Latin her entire career, after graduating from Vassar in 1906. For the last ten years of Maud's life, she and Ada shared her new, smaller house in Woodstock.

A Hungarian shepherd, embroidered by Maud in the 1960s.

without charm"—until it was transformed by Maud.[79] She continued her interest in gardening and also worked on original embroidery as well as on a handful of book projects.

> The house where I now live is a tiny simple house on a village street but with a flower garden encircled by a low brick wall and with one large apple tree with golden apples. I have a view of a nearby mountain and over my mountain, stars with infinity for background, give me faith and peace.
>
> From the day the first seed catalogue arrives until the first frost my interest is in my garden with time out for modeling in clay, embroidering pictures in yarn and at my desk playing with ideas for another book for children which yet has not worked out to my satisfaction.[80]

She began several projects, leaving detailed dummies and typescripts. She enlisted family to help her with research on "Who's Who in Fairylore." Her niece Mitzi plumbed the resources of the Library of Congress, while Maud worked in the Vassar Library; they were looking for anything they could find on leprechauns, elves, trolls, pixies, brownies and all other manner of special folk for what was intended as an encyclopedic compendium. "Jasper's Camel," for which there is both typescript and an early-stage dummy, is marked in Maud's handwriting, "A book that Miska always wanted to make." It is another story with a biblical theme, told from the viewpoint of a camel that was with the Magi when they went to see the newborn Jesus. None of these projects was ever completed. Maud always had said that while she liked starting projects, Miska was the finisher, and on a questionnaire for *Horn Book Magazine* she wrote, "Miska and I worked so closely that joy is gone when working alone."[81]

Maud remained active for the ten years she lived after Miska's death—still rich in friends and beloved in Woodstock. A sketchbook she made during that time is full of delicate watercolors of the changing seasons, the birds outside her window, sunrises and sunsets, and Woodstock's iconic Overlook Mountain, which Maud could see from her little house. She died in Ravenna, Ohio, in 1971, surrounded by her family.

My Mountain, one of several small, delicate watercolors painted by Maud in the 1960s. This 1968 work depicts a view from her little house in the village. The mountain is Overlook, an emblem of Woodstock, and much painted.

CHAPTER 2

Hardworking Artists Illustrating the Work of Others

The Petersham pictures wear well. They have new tricks for second and third lookings.

— Carl Sandburg, commenting on
the Petershams' lively illustrations
for his *Rootabaga Stories* [1]

After Maud and Miska met at the International Art Service in New York, Miska took Maud under his wing in a courtship-cum-mentorship that culminated in their marriage on April 17, 1917. Miska traveled upstate on weekends and got to know Maud's family—parents and sisters, as well as the beloved Auntie (Celia Jane Sisson). Maud said that although she had a year of formal art training at the New York School of Fine and Applied Art, she learned more from Miska than in all her other training. "I had several English courses in college and then one easy-going year in art school. My real training came when I started working with Miska who had graduated from the Budapest Art Academy after several years of intensive training in different forms of art." [2]

When they married, Miska had been earning his keep as a commercial artist since arriving in America five years earlier, in 1912; Maud

had done the cover, endpapers and title page for one book, a poetry anthology edited by Kenneth Grahame. It was the prolific artist and illustrator Willy Pogány, a friend of Miska's and a fellow Hungarian, who opened the door to the world of children's book illustration. Pogány had numerous commissions, many from Macmillan, and asked Miska if he could help him out by taking on a part of the overflow. [3] Frederic G. Melcher, long-time editor of *Publishers Weekly*, wrote, "It was Willy Pogány who turned over to this inspired pair the commission for a book for children which he did not have time to finish, thus turning over to the delights of children, genius in line and color which might have tarried longer in the realm of advertising art." [4] This was a big break, but it was the Petershams' versatility, dependability and attention to detail that ensured that they would never in their lives be without work.

Maud and Miska worked together as artists for twelve years before they tried their hand at

Maud and Miska, sporting two of the costumes they collected on their travels. Authentic folk garb showed up in their carefully researched illustrations. The Petersham grandchildren and their young neighborhood friends enjoyed a rainy afternoon of play when the costume trunk would come out.

writing as well as illustrating, and they continued to illustrate the work of others throughout their long careers. In the busy early years between 1917 and 1929, they provided artwork for at least thirty books as well as for children's magazines such as *St. Nicholas*. Although they worked on high-profile original works, such as Carl Sandburg's *Rootabaga Stories* and Margery Clark's groundbreaking picture book *The Poppy Seed Cakes*, their bread and butter was textbooks and books in series that required hundreds of illustrations. They continued to illustrate the work of other writers through 1955, well after they had attained a secure place in the world of children's picture books. Among the nineteen books they illustrated between 1930 and 1955 were fresh editions of classics—*Pinocchio*, *Rip Van Winkle*, *Heidi*—and original work by Macmillan and Doubleday authors. The Petershams were called upon throughout their career for their skillful illustra-

tion of religious themes. *Told Under the Christmas Tree* (1948) and *In Clean Hay* (1953) were among the last of the many religious stories they treated, starting with 1919's *A Wonderful Night*.

The sheer volume of work involved in illustrating these titles cannot be overestimated. They produced artwork for at least two titles every year, many of which included more than a hundred images, scores of black-and-white line drawings and a handful of full-page, full-color paintings or prints. Maud's aunt (Auntie), an integral member of their household, noted as early as 1920 that the Petershams had so much work "making pictures for school books" that they had to enlist the help of Sam Wiley, a Woodstock artist and illustrator. Sam became a lasting friend and partner; Auntie wrote in 1941, "Sam is still with us, always ready when needed, faithful and true, splendid as a friend and companion."[5]

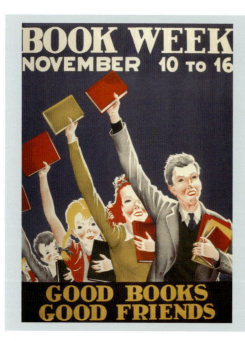

Poster executed by the Petershams for Children's Book Week, November 10–16, 1940. Every year, a distinguished illustrator produces a poster for this national celebration, which was cofounded by the Boy Scouts, *Publishers Weekly* and the American Library Association. This was the second such poster by the Petershams; they did their first one in 1931.

The Burgeoning World of Children's Books

The 1920s were a time of rapid growth and change in the American book industry, and an especially exciting time for children's publishing. New educational theories, a growing population and the development of more efficient printing processes combined to offer publishers a promising market.

In 1919 the American Booksellers Association and the American Library Association (ALA) jointly established Children's Book Week. This annual celebration focused public attention on the importance of good children's books and child literacy, and provided a gathering point for publishers, booksellers and the librarians who were becoming so influential in the children's book trade. The 1922 inauguration of the ALA's Newbery Medal for the most distinguished children's book of the year intensified the spotlight on this growing literature.

Against this background of increasing interest and demand, editors and publishers welcomed the Petershams' expertise and diligence. In a 1926 letter, Edward K. Robinson of Ginn & Company, a textbook publisher, expressed appreciation for the Petershams' businesslike ways and urged them to commit themselves to future projects:

> The last of the drawings for the arithmetic arrived this morning, and we are very much pleased with them. They are exactly what we hoped they might be; there was not one disappointing drawing in the whole lot, and many exceeded our expectations. Many thanks for the careful attention you gave them, and also for the promptness with which you completed them. Miss Wood is making the count of the total num-

The last of three posters the Petershams produced for Children's Book Week—this one in 1946. The theme here refers to attempts to repair wartime bridge-burning.

There were many bridges in Budapest, of stone and iron which when I was a young boy always stretched between us and good times. One bridge was guarded by two enormous stone lions with vacant faces and open mouth, but what was more to be dreaded was a tall house with an ogre in uniform standing at the door demanding the pennies for crossing over the bridge which connected Pest and old Buda. I lived in Pest and the swimming beach or the Turkish bath, where my friends and I liked to play, were over the bridge on the Buda side. . . . Sometimes the motormen would give us a break and some nearly broke our heart. . . .

So you see in my life I have used many bridges real and otherwise and I am proud to be classed as a builder of bridges. — Miska's notes for a speech for Children's Book Week festivities in 1946

ber you have done, and will have a check sent to you promptly. . . . I am going to ask if you will reserve an indefinite period for us, for I think we shall have several books which we should like very much to have you illustrate. . . . I will agree to make the prices entirely satisfactory to you.[6]

"Fairy Godmother" and Other Champions

If Willy Pogány unlocked the door to children's publishing for Maud and Miska, it was May Massee who opened it wide, to a whole world of possibilities in this new and rapidly growing field. Massee was the first editor of juvenile books at Doubleday, recruited from the editorship of the prestigious ALA *Booklist* in 1922 to head up a brand new department of young people's books, the second such in the business. She had begun her career as one of the new breed of librarians specializing in work with children and was well regarded in the worlds of children's libraries and children's bookshops. "Coming to Doubleday, she was already a personage."[7] Massee understood the new role that children's books might play in the complex times following World War I. Despite the isolationist trend in American society (evidenced, for example, by the Palmer Raids, the rise of the Ku Klux Klan and the refusal of Congress to ratify the League of Nations Treaty), Massee had a firmly internationalist approach. And she educated herself diligently about the innovations in printing processes and book production, forging close relationships with printers that enabled her to take a bold approach to color, format and design.

Massee's eye for talent was working overtime when she first encountered the work of Maud and Miska Petersham. Maud's account of their first meeting credits Massee with much of their success:

May Massee was a fairy godmother to Miska and to me . . . as well to many other young would-be artists and authors of the late 1920s. . . . At that time we were living in the Village freelancing and struggling to keep our heads above water even though we paid but $35 a month for our apartment. . . . One lucky day I ventured to Doubleday, Doran & Co. I was directed to the office of the juvenile books and here I found no awesome editor behind the desk, but a warm, friendly, charming person with whom I instantly felt at ease. It was May Massee. Thoughtfully and slowly she looked over the samples of our work—and then smiled and said I am interested in these and I would like to meet Miska, too. . . .[8]

Massee gave the couple many commissions throughout the 1920s, almost all of them titles with an international setting. Their brilliant and innovative illustrations and design for Margery Clark's 1924 *The Poppy Seed Cakes* secured them a place in the hall of fame. "*The Poppy Seed Cakes* was the first book where they let us use color," Miska remembered in a letter, "but only flat colors, no color separation. Even then they had to print 12,000 copies to pay for the cost of plates, a number they argued would never sell. But finally when they saw the pictures they took a chance, and sold it out by Christmas—in less than 6 months."[9] This book showcases the Petershams' sense of humor, their sense of color and their understanding of overall book design. Leonard S. Marcus in *Minders of Make-Believe*, his definitive history of children's books in America, notes, "The Petershams' books were widely praised as touchstones of the new American picture book."[10] Massee later shepherded Maud and Miska's first writing effort through the publication process, and she would encourage them throughout the first two decades of their lives as artists.

May Massee (1883–1966) was founding editor of two children's departments at major publishers, first Doubleday and then Viking. With Louise Seaman Bechtel and Bertha Mahony Miller, she was a leader in American children's book publishing in the twentieth century. Before entering the publishing business, Massee was a librarian; she served as editor of the ALA's *Booklist* from 1913 to 1922.

No editor of her pioneering generation would touch Massee's record of success, especially in the realm of picture books. — Leonard S. Marcus

Maud and Miska did not work exclusively with Massee and Doubleday. Many of their early illustration commissions were for texts and series published by Macmillan, Pogány's publisher, under the leadership of the formidable pioneer of children's publishing Louise Seaman Bechtel. Bechtel was head of the very first children's book department in an American publishing firm, appointed in 1919 and remaining in the post until 1934. A Vassar graduate (1915) and classmate of Maud's younger sister, Winifred, she credited an unnamed Vassar classmate with getting the president of Macmillan to hire her.[11] During her long career, Bechtel reviewed books for the *New York Herald Tribune* and was editor of *Horn Book Magazine*. While not an intimate friend of the Petershams, Bechtel remained collegially in touch with them. She praises their work in a note of congratulations around the time of their 1946 Caldecott Medal for *The Rooster Crows*: "You have done so many lovely books, and each of them might have had a private hurrah from me to you. . . ."[12]

Maud and Miska's relationship with Macmillan would continue throughout their lives, and they were close friends as well as colleagues of Doris Patee, successor to Bechtel and head of children's books from 1934 to 1962. Patee was editor of many of the books the Petershams wrote and illustrated during this time, including their Caldecott Honor and Medal books.

Bertha Mahony (later Miller) was another in the small group of pioneering women who championed the Petershams early in their career. She opened the Book Shop for Boys and Girls in 1916 in Boston and held considerable sway in the development of American children's literature and the business of children's books. In 1924 she founded *Horn Book Magazine*, a publication that is revered to this day. The Book Shop was publisher of *Guld: The Cavern King*, written by Mary L. B. Branch and illustrated by the Petershams. Mahony wrote an admiring note to Maud in 1918: "Yes, the illustrations arrived promptly and the plates are now on their way to our printer in Bingham-

Bertha Mahony (later Miller) opened the Book Shop for Boys and Girls in 1916 in Boston. She was an important figure in the development of children's books in America. She later founded *Horn Book Magazine*, which is still vigorous today. In 1918 Miller published *Guld: The Cavern King*, by Mary L. B. Branch, illustrated by the Petershams.

ton. We are delighted with them. We knew that they would be lovely but they go even beyond our expectations."[13]

An Author's Appreciation: The illustrations are perfect!

While it was the editors and publishers who ensured that Maud and Miska had plenty of work during their early years, the comments of authors are illuminating as well. Many wrote how pleased they were with the way in which the Petershams enlivened their words.

Writing from Vermont in 1923, the author Frances Ross alludes to how good illustration can greatly increase the effect of a book, and even enhance the author's own appreciation for it: "I simply cannot tell you how thrilled and how excited I was when my manuscript for *Reading to Find Out* came back from Macmillan's with your darling illustrations. They are simply perfect! And I want to thank you again and again for making my book so artistic that I am filled with pride every time I see it."[14]

Mabel G. La Rue, a Normal School teacher and textbook author, wrote to Maud in 1926:

Last week I received from Macmillan sheets containing the most charming illustrations for *The Billy Bang Book*. They have afforded me hours of joy. One comes to think of the characters she puts in a book as very real, and I, like a fond mother with her children, should be grieved to see the Rabbit, the Squirrel, the Robin, or any other, represented in a way that I did not want him to look. But you and Mr. Petersham always surprise me by making better pictures than I had imagined.[15]

While using the slightly formal tone of the clergyman, James Snowden, writing in 1919, is unequivocal in his valuing of the Petershams' work on his book:

> I wish to express to the two artists who illustrated my little book *A Wonderful Night* my appreciation of the fine work they have done. They have happily caught and expressed the idea of the book at every point, and their initial letters of the chapters are especially good as they are all different and each one aptly illustrates the point of the chapter. They have added much to the value and beauty of the book.[16]

Mary L. B. Branch, author of the 1918 *Guld: The Cavern King,* does not try for restraint:

> How long I have had to wait to see my own book! But now returning here I see the copy last sent and also the one sent to New London which had been forwarded. So I have it and I am delighted, *wildly* delighted, I thought of telegraphing in those very words. My daughter was with me, we found Guld himself, his *true self,* in each one. I had not allowed myself to be anxious, but I did hope Guld's pictures would look something like him, and they look exactly like him. It is wonderful. And the three situations are a perfect choice. Those artists have not missed a point. I feel radiant.[17]

After 1929, when they published their first written-and-illustrated book, they slowed down their efforts in illustrating the texts of others. However, this work never stopped entirely: The 1930s saw pictures for *Heidi, Pinocchio,* the Lambs' *Tales From Shakespeare* and many original books. Their ability to choose just the right part of the action to illustrate, and to capture character—even in animals—was much sought after. The last book for which they served as illustrators was Miriam E. Mason's *Miss Posy Longlegs,* published in 1955. Mason chose the Petershams because of her delight with their illustrations for a previous book, *Susannah: The Pioneer Cow.* "Susannah and the Waynes look just exactly the way I wanted them to look," she wrote in 1941, "and Susannah is especially satisfactory because you have managed to convey in the pictures just the spirit which I had in writing the story."[18]

Widening Reputation

As early as 1925, the Petershams were considered authorities of the aesthetics behind children's illustration, as well as expert practitioners. The *Elementary English Review,* an academic journal, solicited an article by Maud. Her tone is light but confident. She critiques the famous illustrators Rackham, Dulac, Boutet de Monvel and Ten-

The Book House for Children was a Chicago publishing company founded by Olive Beaupré Miller to bring the classics and an international sensibility to young children. The publisher actually sold "houses" for children to store their books. The Petershams illustrated two titles in the "My Travelship" series (in this picture, the tall books at the left).

niel, and outlines her own criteria for what makes for good book art. "An illustration should have . . . story, color, action, and fun—but it should also be beautiful in design and line and should have feeling. The design should be simple and the line sensitive." A tall order, perhaps, but for a worthy cause—early exposure to fine artwork in books will ensure finer tastes when one is grown up, and "the child who is not learning to see beauty is losing an inestimable source of happiness."[19]

During this period they developed their life-long devotion to painstaking research. "We did have fun working on books for children for it often meant travel with sketch book in hand. Our work for The Book House took us to France and to Holland."[20] Maud refers to *Nursery Friends From France* (1925) and *Tales Told in Holland* (1926), both by Olive Beaupré Miller. Many of their extensive sketches of people, costume, buildings and natu-ral landscape are extant. Numerous publishers called on the Petershams to illustrate books with an international flavor. A few standouts among these are Marguerite Clément's *Where Was Bobby?*, 1928, a tale of a brother and sister in France, and *The Magic Doll of Roumania*, 1929.

The Petershams were clearly among the leading children's illustrators in the 1920s. In the 1929 exhaustive annotated bibliography *Realms of Gold in Children's Books* they are represented by more entries than any other illustrator except the legendary Arthur Rackham.[21] This was before they had written *Miki*, though after *The Poppy Seed Cakes* was in the bookstores. By the time Maud and Miska ventured to write their own books, they were well known and highly regarded by the librarians, editors, publishers and reviewers who would shape children's literature in the twentieth century.

Important Books in This Chapter

Good English, by Henry Seidel Canby and John Baker Opdycke. Macmillan, 1918

Guld: The Cavern King, by Mary L. B. Branch. Bookshop for Boys and Girls, Women's Educational and Industrial Union, 1918

A Wonderful Night, by James Henry Snowden. Macmillan, 1919

Tales of Enchantment From Spain, by Elsie Spicer Eells. Harcourt, Brace, 1920

Rootabaga Stories, by Carl Sandburg. Harcourt, Brace, 1922

Tales From Shakespeare, by Charles and Mary Lamb. Macmillan, 1923

The Poppy Seed Cakes, by Margery Clark [Mary E. Clark and Margaret Closey Quigley]. Doubleday, Page, 1924

Nursery Friends From France, by Olive Beaupré Miller. Book House for Children, 1925

Tales Told In Holland, by Olive Beaupré Miller. Book House for Children, 1926

The Billy Bang Book, by Mabel G. La Rue. Macmillan, 1927

Children of the Mountain Eagle, by Elizabeth Cleveland Miller. Doubleday, Doran, 1927

Where Was Bobby? by Marguerite Clément. Doubleday, Doran, 1928

The Magic Doll of Roumania, by Marie, Queen of Roumania. Frederick A. Stokes, 1929

Pran of Albania, by Elizabeth Cleveland Miller. Doubleday, Doran, 1930

Heidi, by Johanna Spyri. Garden City, 1932

Pinocchio, by Carlo Collodi. Garden City, 1932

Albanian Wonder Tales, by Post Wheeler. Doubleday, Doran, 1936

Susannah: The Pioneer Cow, by Miriam E. Mason. Macmillan, 1941

Told Under the Christmas Tree, Association for Childhood Education. Macmillan, 1948

Rip Van Winkle, by Washington Irving. Macmillan, 1951

In Clean Hay, by Eric P. Kelly. Macmillan, 1953

Miss Posy Longlegs, by Miriam E. Mason. Macmillan, 1955

THE STORK
Ooievaar

Storky-lork,
Storky-stork,
Steal a twig,
Stork loves babies small and big.

A page from "The Stork" in *Tales Told in Holland*. This was the second of two books the Petershams illustrated for the Book House international series.

Dear Mr. Petersham:

I have just received the copy of Tales Told in Holland *which I ordered from The Book House for Children in Chicago. I have immensely enjoyed the pictures which you made for this book. They are most attractive. It must have been a great delight to you and Mrs. Petersham to gather in Holland the material that you used in these pictures . . .* — E. K. Robinson, Publisher, Ginn & Company

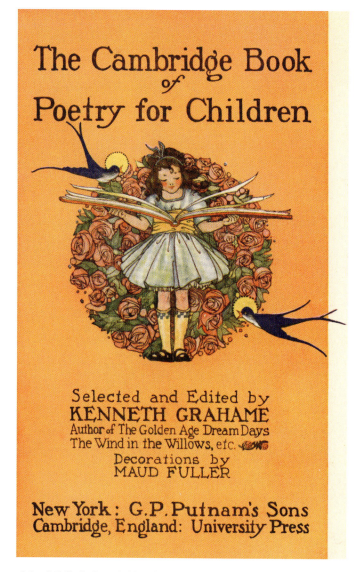

Maud Fuller's first children's illustration commission was for the cover, this title page, and endpapers for *The Cambridge Book of Poetry for Children*, selected and edited by none other than the author of *The Wind in the Willows*. The good cheer and solid design sense that characterize later Petersham work are already apparent here. Note the swallowtail extending beyond the frame of the picture, and also the giant book, open and ready to fly from the arms of the child.

I learned little in art school, but Miska has been my severe and thorough teacher. — Maud

GOOD ENGLISH

BY

HENRY SEIDEL CANBY
AND
JOHN BAKER OPDYCKE

ILLUSTRATIONS BY
MAUD AND MISKA PETERSHAM

THE MACMILLAN COMPANY, PUBLISHERS
NEW YORK MCMXXI

AROUND THE CAMPFIRE.

The title page and an illustration from *Good English*, published by Macmillan in 1918, one of many textbooks the Petershams illustrated early in their career. This exhaustive text is 390 pages long and is scattered with numerous illustrations, both large and small.

Authors of the books that the Petershams illustrated were very appreciative of Maud and Miska's ability to bring their words to life. One wrote, *I am delighted*, wildly *delighted. . . . Those artists have not missed a point. I feel radiant.*

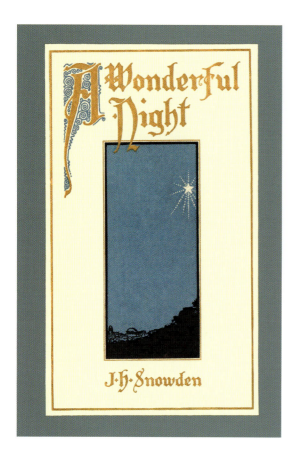

Cover, frontispiece and an initial
capital for a chapter head from
A Wonderful Night (Macmillan, 1919).

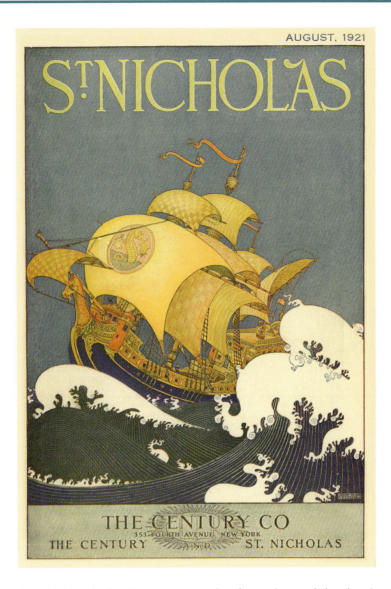

AUGUST, 1921

ST·NICHOLAS

THE CENTURY CO
353-FOURTH AVENUE NEW YORK
THE CENTURY — AND — ST. NICHOLAS

The Petershams did not do the Christmas cover referred to in the note below, but they did create two *St. Nicholas* covers in 1921, including the one pictured here. This venerable magazine provided good exposure for illustrators, especially those just starting out. It set an early standard for taking children seriously. Founding editor Mary Mapes Dodge, author of *Hans Brinker*, was at the helm from 1873 to 1905. She recruited such writers as Louisa May Alcott, Rudyard Kipling and Mark Twain to its pages. *St. Nicholas* was deemed "the dominating influence affecting for good the production of children's literature in America."

*Dear Mrs. P., I have been wondering whether you and Mr. Petersham would have any suggestions for a Christmas cover. . . . The October cover was worth waiting for. It delighted me as much as it will the children. — Frances Marshall, *St. Nicholas* magazine*

OPPOSITE "The balloons floated and filled the sky." Frontispiece from *Rootabaga Stories*, by Carl Sandburg (Harcourt, Brace, 1922)

We are all delighted with the frontispiece. It is perfect. — D. C. Brace

The Petershams sure outran their own records in that colored frontispiece. It keys the best gayety of the book . . . — Carl Sandburg

Illustration for "The Huckabuck Family," in *Rootabaga Pigeons.*

And it seems to me the Petersham pictures wear well. . . . They have new tricks for second and third lookings. — Carl Sandburg

TOP A chapter heading for "Poker Face the Baboon and Hot Dog the Tiger," in *Rootabaga Stories.*

BOTTOM Chapter-ending illustration for "How the Animals Lost Their Tails and Got Them Back Traveling From Philadelphia to Medicine Hat," in *Rootabaga Stories.*

I didn't notice till yesterday the tail of [Poker Face the Baboon] hung on a hook. — Carl Sandburg, in a letter to Harcourt, Brace, publishers of *Rootabaga Stories*, which the Petershams illustrated

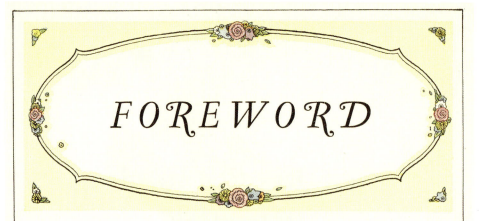

FOREWORD

THESE little *chansons*, which take the place of nursery rhymes in France, have been beloved by generations of French children, for most of them are at least a hundred years old. They come to America, bearing the lively, varied rhythms, now gay and bounding in merriment, now sweet and tender, which can well up from no single writer, but only from the hearts of a whole people. There is more of the real France in these rhymes than in volumes of more learned books. And what a kaleidoscope of French life—shepherds and shepherdesses, now from the dainty fancy of a Watteau, now from the rugged reality of a Jules Breton, peasants and princes, citizens and villagers, ploughmen and sailors, lawyers and millers, carpenters and blacksmiths, duchesses and beggars! Now one wanders in shops and city squares, where dames of Paris sweep all day; in a moment, *presto!* there is the countryside—flowery meadows, green fields, and forests, chateaux, thatched cottages and Gothic church spires. This is France and this is the French *chanson*.

May the rhythm of these poems find an echo in the hearts of the children of America!

The Foreword for *Nursery Friends From France*. The Petershams traveled to Europe to research their pictures for this book, one of two volumes they illustrated for the Book House international series. Note the characteristic illuminated initial capital; several authors and reviewers commented with pleasure on these capitals.

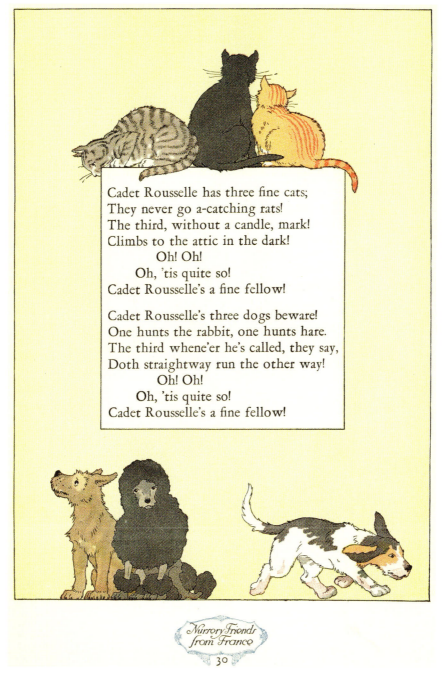

Cadet Rousselle has three fine cats;
They never go a-catching rats!
The third, without a candle, mark!
Climbs to the attic in the dark!
          Oh! Oh!
     Oh, 'tis quite so!
Cadet Rousselle's a fine fellow!

Cadet Rousselle's three dogs beware!
One hunts the rabbit, one hunts hare.
The third whene'er he's called, they say,
Doth straightway run the other way!
          Oh! Oh!
     Oh, 'tis quite so!
Cadet Rousselle's a fine fellow!

Nursery Friends from France

30

A page-framing illustration the Petershams did for *Nursery Friends From France*.
It demonstrates their whimsical enjoyment of animals.

and carried him in to his fine feather bed.

TO HIS FINE FEATHER BED

May Massee was editor for most of the Petershams' important books between 1922 and 1934, including *The Poppy Seed Cakes* by Margery Clark. This two-page spread displays classic Petersham elements: the illustrations as container for the text, a cozy bed, folk design elements and bright colors.

On these pages and the two pages following, illustrations from *The Poppy Seed Cakes*.

The Poppy Seed Cakes was a milestone . . . for children's books. A charming story with an old world setting and flavor, it was illustrated in the colorful peasant style that came to be recognized as pure Petersham, and its decorative borders and endpapers showed their feeling for good book design. — Anita Silvey

Goose—one of several motifs in the book.

"Auntie Katushka brought a huge bag filled with presents." Bright
colors, folk motifs and a sense of humor—Petersham hallmarks.

"The Green goose tugged at the fine feather bed."

his long red beak.

"Stop, Green Goose!" said Andrew-shek, "and I will give you one of Auntie Katushka's poppy seed cakes."

"A poppy seed cake!" the green goose quacked in delight. "I love nice little poppy seed cakes! Give me one and you shall have your feather bed."

But one poppy seed cake could not

A page of text showing layout and decorative borders.

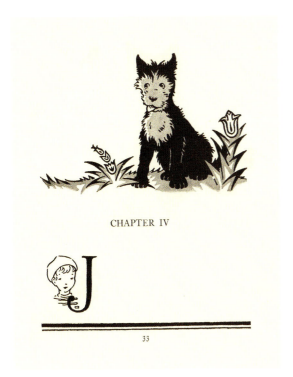

CHAPTER IV

J

33

119

Where Was Bobby?, by Marguerite Clément (Doubleday, 1928), is a 151-page chapter book describing the adventures of two children and their pets. "Bobby" is a small terrier. The book is chock full of color and black-and-white illustrations. Shown here are cover art (left), mimicking the red door of the Petershams' own house in Woodstock; two pages exhibiting their approach to overall layout design; and one of the book's full-page color illustrations captioned, "Mummy sent up dull food."

The Magic Doll of Roumania, by Marie, Queen of Roumania, is typical of the many books with international themes that the Petershams illustrated. Shown here is one of the full-page illustrations. A colorful figure, Marie was a granddaughter of Queen Victoria; she married Prince Ferdinand of Roumania when she was seventeen. Ferdinand ascended the throne in 1914. Marie was a staunch supporter of the Allies in World War I and served with the Red Cross.

None of us like to be forgotten, and I am no exception to this rule. So I began to wonder what I could do in order that you should remember me. And so it was that I decided to write this story for you—a simple story, with songs and verses in it, which I hope all of you will enjoy.

And because I am Queen of a far-away country which I know will interest you—a country full of poetry and pictures, of old customs and quaint habits handed down through long generations from father to son, from mother to daughter—I have placed my story in Roumania and among the peasants, for it is they who guard the past. — Marie, Queen of Roumania, in her Preface to *The Magic Doll of Roumania,* written after she visited the United States in the 1920s

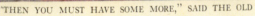
"THEN YOU MUST HAVE SOME MORE," SAID THE OLD

THE BOY REFUSED IT WHEN SHE OFFERED IT TO HIM.

Two of the Petershams' illustrations for Johanna Spyri's *Heidi* (Garden City, 1932). Miska and Maud illustrated many iconic titles in addition to *Heidi*, including the Lambs' *Tales From Shakespeare* (Macmillan, 1923); Carlo Collodi's *Pinocchio* (Garden City, 1932); and Washington Irving's *Rip Van Winkle* (Macmillan, 1951).

We make mistakes too, where the author could place the blame on us as artists. We once illustrated "Heidi"—I had always thought of Heidi with flaxen hair and we made her that way in our pictures—after the finished book was in our hands to my chagrin I discovered the author's Heidi was described as having hair of black. A child doesn't forgive you for mistakes like this. — Maud

This illustration is from *The World of Music: Tuning Up*, a textbook published by Ginn & Company in 1936. The Petershams received commissions from all quarters, as their reputation grew throughout the worlds of both textbook and trade publishing for solid, professional work delivered on time.

The cow in this picture jumped over the moon but "liked it so well up there that she never came back down!"

It is from Miriam E. Mason's *Miss Posy Longlegs*, illustrated by the Petershams.

This image is from *Susannah: The Pioneer Cow*, also written by Miriam E. Mason and illustrated by the Petershams (Macmillan, 1941).

I want to tell you how much I enjoyed the pictures you made of my "Susannah" in our book which is just finished. . . . I wanted [the images of] Susannah to look entirely true to life, Susannah being a real cow who gives milk and looks like a cow, yet besides being a cow, I wanted her to have a well defined personality and the power of feeling many moods. — Miriam E. Mason

CHAPTER 3

All Ours

Early Picture Books, 1929–1934

At first we illustrated books written by others, but often we found no place in the text that lent itself to illustration, so we decided to plan a book of our own with both pictures and text.

— Maud Petersham[1]

I just adore "Miki"–it's by all odds the loveliest picture book ever made in this country–and I want to talk to you about the next one.

— May Massee,
the Petershams' editor at Doubleday[2]

Between 1929 and 1934 the Petershams illustrated *and* wrote four big, beautiful and groundbreaking books, all midwifed by May Massee. Each is autobiographical, highlighting an element of their lives. Indeed, Maud once wrote, "Anyone who enjoys our work can really feel very well acquainted with us."[3]

With May's encouragement, Maud and Miska devised the story for *Miki*. They laid out a dummy, illustrations first, and some text. The Petershams fully expected that the text would have to be rewritten by "an author of children's books"[4]–but not themselves. May's quick response put that notion to rest: "We all love MIKI, as of course I knew we would. The text needs very little editing, and I think we can do that ourselves . . . you write so naturally that

nobody would want to change very much." The rest of her letter outlines the complicated business of creating a picture book, making it all seem quite simple:

I think that you should plan out all of your text right away and send that up to me so that we can set it up for you. You can't be sure about your drawings until you have that set up so that you can make it up just as it's going to be. From the dummy it looks as though you wanted two colors on one side of the sheet and five colors on the other side: red, blue, yellow, green and black, with a Benday of the red. Do you think a 64-page book will be long enough? That is what I'll try to plan . . . We'll try to have lithography which would give us all the colors and then we will try making plates and doing our own printing with flat colors which would mean much better paper used and a more workmanlike book.[5]

Miska and Maud outside their home in Woodstock, New York.

Given this optimism and support, it's no wonder that Maud would later write of the Massee magic: "I don't know just what it is that May does to the artists who come to her. Whatever it is, it makes you able to do your best work for her. She gives you a feeling of confidence in her judgment and in your own ability."[6]

A Midlife Autobiography in Picture Books

Miki bears the tantalizing subtitle *The Book of Maud and Miska Petersham*, suggesting that perhaps they thought it would be the only such book. It is named for their young son, who was six years old when the book was published. It is the story of a little boy who—by himself—takes a trip to Hungary and encounters fascinating sights and people and animals. Many of the scenes are vignettes from Miska's childhood, encompassing shepherds on the plain and adventures in the big cities of Buda and Pest. The bright artwork makes direct reference to Hungarian folk conventions. Anita Silvey touts it as a book of many firsts: "*Miki* was the first book the Petershams both illustrated and wrote, the first big colored picture book printed in the United States, and the first of a tide of picture books set in a foreign land."[7]

Three years later came a book based on Maud's childhood, *Auntie and Celia Jane and Miki*. Maud wrote, "My favorite book is *Auntie*, perhaps because it is so personal, the story of those dearest to us."[8] Many of the stories are taken right from Maud's life, and from that of her real-life Auntie, Celia Jane Sisson. Some of the episodes are recounted in Sisson's unpublished autobiography, written in 1941. In the first half of the Petershams' book, "Auntie" is a young woman who lives with her Quaker father and delights in Celia Jane's summertime visits. Celia Jane hides in the hayloft at the end of one summer, so her parents have to leave her with Auntie all year. Maud had spent summers with the real Auntie and her Quaker grandfather. Sisson's autobiography includes a similar real-life episode when Maud hid in the hayloft and ended up living with her for the next six years. In the second half of the Petershams' book, Auntie is an old woman, a special and important person to the character Miki, a boy of about ten. In real life, Auntie lived with Maud and Miska. She was a central part of their young son's life, running the household and caring for Miki when his parents were off on their travels. "A new book by the Petershams always means a real thrill for me," wrote Olive Beaupré Miller, an author whose books they illustrated. "The humor, the beauty of color, line, and design in 'Auntie and Celia Jane and Miki' gave me a very happy evening indeed."[9]

If *Miki* is Miska's story and *Auntie* is Maud's, *Get-A-Way and Háry János* refers to some of their shared interests and adventures. *Get-A-Way* is the tale of two worn-out toys who escape the scrap heap and land in a magical place where toys can become as new. Maud and Miska collected toys from many lands during their travels; some of these appear as characters in the pages of *Get-A-Way*. The character of Háry János comes from a nineteenth-century Hungarian novel and a 1926 opera by the Hungarian composer Zoltán Kodály. One reviewer saw similarities with Margery Williams' 1922 *Velveteen Rabbit*: "I know of but one scene in a story book for little children that moves me in the same way as this book: the moment in the deathless 'Velveteen Rabbit,' when the rabbit, having helped a little boy through scarlet fever . . . goes leaping gladly toward some paradise well earned by good toys. Here, in the Petershams' best book, is that rainbow paradise complete."[10]

May Massee moved from Doubleday to Viking during the development of *Get-A-Way and Háry János*, and the Petershams made the move with her.[11] Her hastily handwritten note to them when she received the final illustrations is characteristically encouraging, although it alludes to a painstaking process of development: "They're simply perfect. . . . You are making one of the great picture books of the world—and of any time—there's never been a book that made toys as real and as important as they are in the child's world—this does it—it's been an awful pull I know but a grand one—Love from me."[12]

The following year saw the last of these early books written by the Petershams and edited by Massee. *Miki and Mary: Their Search for Treasures* is a tale of two youngsters off to faraway lands in Europe and around the Mediterranean. One of the things many people remember about this book is the notable absence of parents, as in *Miki*. Several adults who had been well acquainted with *Miki and Mary* as children have commented on the independence of these pre-pubescent youths as they set off on their adventures.[13] Miki is again patterned on Maud and Miska's son, who was eleven when this book was published, while Mary is based on his cousin Mitzi Byrd (Maud's niece), who spent many summers and other long stretches with the Petersham family.

Developments in Color Lithography

This was a yeasty time in children's book publishing, not only with the emergence of bold and imaginative editors, but also with the development of new processes in color printing. Maud and Miska worked in close partnership with printers throughout their careers, and in some cases helped to develop new techniques. Charles Stringer, the printer for *Miki* and *Auntie*, developed a process that enabled cost-effective full-color printing, a method that was used by many of the important children's publishers of the time, including May Massee's Doubleday and Louise Seaman Bechtel's Macmillan. Bill and Lillian Glaser perfected methods of color separation for lithography using zinc or glass plates. These techniques enabled a sophisticated use of color with just four inks, reducing costs considerably. The Glasers were the printers for *Get-A-Way* and *Miki and Mary*. The Petershams' partnership with the Glasers would continue throughout their careers, as friends as well as colleagues. Miska, known as a perfectionist, spent long days at the print shop, examining proofs, making corrections, ensuring that everything was ready for the printing of a new book.

There was no precedent for the picture-story books that came into their own in the 1930s, the first decade of lower reproduction costs, those books in which profuse illustrations further interpret the story but do not supplant the text in importance. . . . In a very few years, especially in books for younger children, the artist attained a place of equal importance with the writer. In many cases this necessary partnership of artist and author has stimulated an artist to experiment in writing his own stories.[14]

Maud and Miska were certainly in the right place at the right time: expert and thoughtful editing by Massee combined with the introduction of accessible color printing to showcase their remarkable talents. "No editor of her pioneering generation would touch Massee's record of success, especially in the realm of picture books."[15]

Key Themes and Values

Taken together, these four fine picture books exhibit some of the themes that endure in much of the Petershams' work. Their international perspective shines from every page in both *Miki* books, encouraging very young children to appreciate the customs and history of other peoples. Writing during wartime, seventeen years after the release of *Miki,* Irene Smith Green poignantly describes how knowledge of other peoples could be an effective part of a peace movement:

> When *Miki* was published by Doubleday in 1929, a wave of fresh air breezed through the current picture book modes. At once we knew that our immediate borders included far-off Hungary, stretched there by a book that was honest and gaily child-like. *Miki* is still asked for, slept with, worn to tatters in growing families, and replaced continually in public library Children's Rooms. About two years ago, at the height of the war, the seven-year-old nephew of one of my friends was playing a bombing game with some other children. When it was his turn to play, the city happened to be Budapest. "Oh," she heard him say, "I wouldn't want to bomb Budapest! That's where Miki lives."[16]

Another recurrent theme in the Petershams' books is adventure—with optimism and independence to go along with it. *Miki* sets off by himself, without parents, and embarks on another adventure with the younger Mary. Both children are enterprising, open to new experiences and brave in the face of danger. And they both remember to bring presents home to their families. The underlying message here is that, while families are very important, one of their tasks is to prepare children to face the world on their own.

In *Auntie,* the value of extended and intergenerational families is unquestioned: Celia Jane is one of many children, but parents do not have to shoulder the whole burden of nurturing their young—her busy mother and father can rely on a wide circle to help her find her place in the world. Maud and Miska's household operated along these lines. Auntie lived with them her whole life, and Maud's mother and her other sisters spent extended periods with them as well. The Petersham household mirrored *Auntie*'s atmosphere of loving warmth and security combined with encouragement to go off and find one's place in the world. The real-life Miki called his parents by their first names, a practice not uncommon in artistic circles in the 1920s but also indicative of an underlying belief that parents are not the sole nurturers of youngsters—not when there are aunts and cousins and friends to help! In Petersham-land, children can rely on a village to raise them.[17]

The Petershams' love of the natural world is apparent throughout *Miki,* particularly when the boy sleeps with the shepherds under the stars and hears their tales of the zodiac. In *Auntie,* the "mountains that look like elephants" and the beautiful pictures of woodland and meadow are reminiscent of the landscape in the Catskill Mountains, where the Petershams lived.

Miska and Maud in their studio, circa 1933, with part of their collection of international toys. Note that Miska is holding the model for *Get-A-Way*.

A concern for world peace, a wish to bring people of all kinds together rather than split them apart, occupied the couple's minds in the 1930s. They planned a book specifically about peace, as evidenced in a note written by the retired diplomat Norman H. Davis in 1935: "Dear Mrs. Petersham . . . It seems to me that your idea of a peace book for children is an excellent one and I shall be glad to have you give my name as a reference in making application for the Guggenheim Fellowship."[18]

When they wrote *Miki*, both Maud and Miska were seasoned professional artists with fine reputations. *Miki* and the three other picture books they produced between 1929 and 1934 would be the first of more than fifty they illustrated *and* authored over the course of three decades. One reviewer of *Miki and Mary* could barely contain himself: "These two artists are becoming a legend in children's book publishing. Each time they make a book they out-do themselves; each book has an extra something that makes it individual and outstanding."[19]

Important Books in This Chapter

Miki. Doubleday, Doran, 1929
Auntie and Celia Jane and Miki. Doubleday, Doran, 1932
Get-A-Way and Háry János. Viking, 1933
Miki and Mary: Their Search for Treasures. Viking, 1934

MIKI

THIS is a picture of a little boy whose name was Miki.

OPPOSITE Opening page of the narrative of *Miki*, the first book written as well as illustrated by the Petershams. Their son, Miska Fuller Petersham, known as Miki, was born in 1923, and so was five or six when the book was published, in 1929. Characteristic Petersham elements include the bright colors, Miska's hand-lettering in the title and the illuminated initial capital.

Encouraged by May Massee, we laid out a dummy for Miki, working out the pictures first and then a text, which we thought would have to be rewritten by an author of children's books. We sent the dummy to May and her answer was, to our surprise, "We want the book just as it is." — Maud

Illustration from *Miki*. The bright colors and flower motif recall Hungarian folk art.

An adverse criticism from May makes you try harder instead of discouraging you as it does when it comes from some . . .

If you are not an artist or an author and can't know what it is like to have May Massee as a publisher, you can know her as a grand friend. As a publisher and friend they just don't come better. — Maud

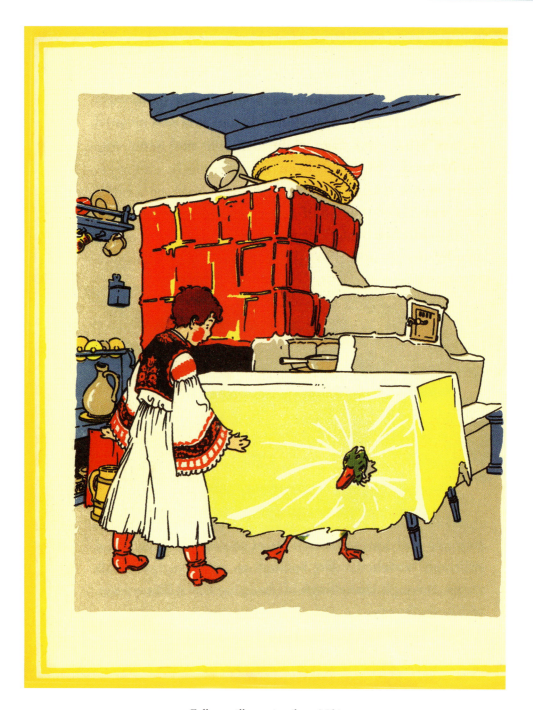

Full-page illustration from *Miki*.

THIS IS THE LAST STORY

NE day a letter came to Miki. In it were three pieces of colored paper with much printing on them. They were tickets. These tickets would take them to Miki's home. One was for Miki, one for Sari, and one for Matyi.

The first page of the last chapter of *Miki*. The Petershams took May Massee's advice about "making the parts of the books quite distinct . . . little chapters." This page includes one of their characteristically rich initial capitals.

In the picture you can see how her father looked.

OPPOSITE Full-page illustration from *Miki*. The young boy looks more fascinated than awed by this robust shepherd in traditional garb.

Miska's grandfather was a shepherd living on the Puszta or Hungarian plains and the small boy greatly admired his tall strong grandfather in his great coat of sheepskin embroidered with bright colors. — Maud

They collected some presents to take home with them—a big bag of paprika, a long round roll of cake filled with poppy seeds, and some other little things.

Then they took the tickets and all went back home to Miki's house.

Full-page illustration from *Miki*. Although there is no sign of parents in *Miki*, he heads home happily, laden with gifts from his visit.

Full-page illustration from *Miki*. Booking passage on a steamship for Miki and the goose and the dog he befriended in Hungary is the work of a single page.

Title page from *Auntie and Celia Jane and Miki*. Where *Miki* is full of images and events from Miska's Hungarian boyhood, *Auntie* recalls Maud's childhood in a family of girls, visiting their grandfather and aunt in the country every summer.

Title page for the Prologue to the first section of *Auntie*. As with *Miki*, this book is divided into chapters—in this case, a "first half" and a "second half," each with a Prologue. In this picture, the main character of the first half, Celia Jane, waves from atop her father's shoulder.

OPPOSITE Illustration from *Auntie*. The accompanying text is autobiographical, with the fictional Celia Jane standing in for Maud:

Grandfather was a great tall man. He was a Quaker, and he wore a big felt hat all the time, even in the house. Celia Jane was always very quiet and very, very good when she came near him.

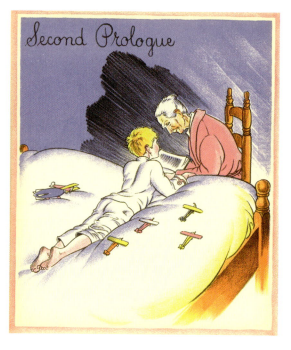

Two-color illustration from *Auntie*. This incident is also taken directly from Maud's life. Auntie wrote about Maud hiding in the hayloft to avoid having to leave her grandfather's house at the end of one summer. Eventually she did get to stay—for six years— just like the little girl in this storybook.

Title page for the second half of *Auntie*. Auntie is now an old woman, but clearly not mired in the past— she shares young Miki's appreciation for air travel, quite a new thing in 1932, when this book was published.

OPPOSITE Full-page illustration from *Auntie*. Miki, of course, is based on Maud and Miska's son. Denny, his friend in the story, was also a real person—Denny Chase, a neighbor of the Petershams in Woodstock and a lifelong friend of Miki's.

"[Miki and Denny] found a pool that was full of fish. The fish looked small, and Miki went all the way back home to get a ruler. They had been told that they were not allowed to keep trout less than six inches long. Miki was going to measure all the fish he caught to make sure."

BACK of Miki's house were hills that looked like sleeping elephants, and down from these hills came a stream full of trout.

One morning Miki and Denny went fishing. To get to this stream, they must pass the tumble-down house of a very cross, a very crabbed old man.

Full page from *Auntie*, showing placement of text and borders. The scenery is a lively and endearing interpretation of the Catskill Mountains landscape near Woodstock, Maud and Miska's hometown.

OPPOSITE Illustration from *Auntie*. The Petershams' reverence for nature often shows in their illustrations. Years later, in *The Peppernuts*, they depicted a scene almost identical to this—a magic cabin in the woods, with leaping fish and fearless deer.

ONE summer Miki lived in a little hunting lodge, 'way in the deep dark woods. Auntie and his Father and Mother were with him. No one else ever came, for the house was so far from the road.

There were tall dark trees all around as far as you could walk. There was a little bright green clearing where the house stood.

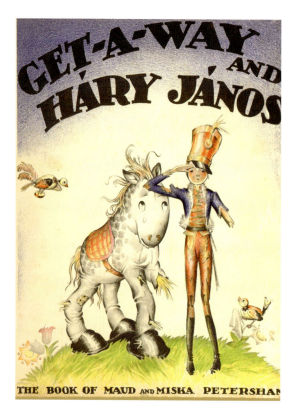

Cover of *Get-A-Way and Háry János*, the third book that Maud and Miska both wrote and illustrated. The models for these illustrations were toys in their collection from around the world. The story is based on a Hungarian folk character, a boastful retired soldier. (The *Háry János Suite*, a frequently performed orchestral piece by the Hungarian-born composer Zoltán Kodály, is based on the same character.)

Illustration from "The House Among the Christmas Trees," chapter 5 of *Get-A-Way.*

OPPOSITE Illustration from "The Horse Race," chapter 6.

Get-A-Way was one of just seventeen books chosen by the American Institute of Graphic Arts for its children's book exhibition in 1934. In the days before the Caldecott Medal, inclusion in this exhibition was a singular honor. Other artists represented in the 1934 show were Peggy Bacon, Wanda Gag, José Clemente Orozco, Edward Steichen and Lynd Ward.

because of the long-handled pan that the omelet was so good, and she
decided to take one home to her mother. Miki had a little French flag
he had found here and he tied this to the long handle of the pan.

The round world on the cover of *Miki and Mary* is a common visual theme for the Petershams. The Miki and Mary characters are based on the Petershams' son and his cousin, Mary (later "Mitzi") Byrd, daughter of Maud's sister Winifred. Mary was considered a member of the Petersham family, spending entire summers with them in Woodstock.

On this round world of ours there are lots of places more interesting than books—castles which you thought were just flat pictures become real and you can walk over the moats and climb up into high towers. You can try foods that look and taste like nothing you have ever known and can see people wearing clothes which you cannot even call by name. You may have to sleep in queer high beds with feather pillows for your cover, but it is fun to wake up in a room full of strange-looking furniture . . . — Maud, "Traveling in Picture Book Places," *Young Wings*, November 1934

Illustration of Mont Saint Michel from *Miki and Mary*. The description of the tide rushing in to cut off the land bridge is memorable, and a little alarming: "Miki could now see silvery blue water . . . the whole big ocean was chasing them. . . . Faster and faster the horses ran. At last they reached the rocks and the panting horses stopped. [Miki and Mary] didn't wait a minute, but ran over the rocks through the gateway . . . and raced up the steep narrow street of cobblestones."

OPPOSITE This illustration of Venice introduces one of the many short chapters delineating Miki and Mary's travels. In addition to Venice and Mont Saint Michel, they visit Concarneau, the Canary Islands, Athens, Rhodes and Jerusalem.

VENICE

A CITY OF ITALY CALLED
THE QUEEN OF THE SEA

Endpapers from *Miki and Mary*, using a device common in medieval illumination whereby several events are illustrated in one image, creating a kind of storyboard. Here, Miki and Mary move from a boat to a castle turret to an airplane to the inside of a castle keep, predicting their adventures in the story.

The versatile Petershams have scored another triumph in their gorgeously illustrated book . . . Miki and Mary are quite unusual children for our day; without any apparent consultation with their parents, they decide to go forth on a long journey on the ocean which will take them to many ports. The purpose of their trip is to search for treasure and Miki explains to Mary that it will not be at all odd if they should meet up with pirates. Because of the danger of their mission, Miki made a large wooden sword for himself and a small one for Mary. — Davenport Daily Times

CHAPTER 4

Illuminating the Bible for Children

Miska and I feel these are the best books we have ever made—they have our heart and soul in them . . . when we were analyzing the text it came over us again and again how simply marvelous the Bible stories were just as they were told. Even trying to make pictures for them seemed a sacrilege—the only excuse we had was if we gave our very best.

— Maud, undated draft for a speech[1]

Maud and Miska illustrated Bible stories with the kind of care that recalls the reverence of the anonymous scribes and illuminators of centuries ago. In a way, the audiences were similar: In medieval times a great many people were unable to read, and most of the Petershams' audience were too young to read. The Petershams' choice of events to illustrate—their detail and drama—combine to hold a child's interest and perhaps to provoke not only questions but also entreaties to "please read it again." And the pictures stay in our minds. Some adults were recently asked, "What do you remember best about the Petershams' books?" Several immediately mentioned the images in *The Christ Child* and *Stories From the Old Testament*. Typical comments ran from "Every Christmas, I still see the manger scene as Maud and Miska did" to "Everything I know about the Bible I learned from these books."[2]

From the Flood to the Nativity

The first two Bible stories were published by Doubleday, Doran, and shepherded to print by the Petershams' mentor and champion, the editor May Massee. The first was a brightly illustrated retelling of the Noah's Ark story, which was printed in 1930 by Charles Stringer, the same printer who had done so well by *Miki*. *The Ark of Father Noah and Mother Noah* is a story "as seen by Maud and Miska Petersham," not exactly claiming authorship of a tale that comes from Genesis. The tale is told with rollicking humor spiced with great poignancy, as, for example, in the explanation of why the dinosaurs and woolly mammoth were not able to go on the voyage: Father Noah had made the door too small and had not had time to fix it before the rains. The dinosaurs cried. And so did Father Noah. The illustrations are bright and colorful and bold, with many folk art references. Anyone familiar with *The Poppy*

Maud and Miska in 1946, outside their Woodstock home.

Seed Cakes or *Miki* would immediately know that this was the work of the Petershams.

The following year brought *The Christ Child*. Here the pictures are more complex and subtle than those in the *Ark*. These illustrations shine with depth and light. "The reverence and beauty of their pictures . . . make this one of the loveliest of interpretations of the Christmas story for little children,"[3] commented one reviewer. Maud and Miska decided to use the text from the King James Version of the Bible rather than attempt to retell the nativity story in childish words. The title page credits the traditional authors: "as told by Matthew and Luke." The book was widely and well reviewed, at a time when children's literature was just beginning to get the attention of reviewers. The *New York Times* commented, "The animals, from the small lamb . . . to the splendid camels of the Wise Men, interest and please children. Lambs especially, as these artists draw them, have a gentle humor that is very winning, and the tiny, exquisite flowers have the same youthful quality."[4] Maud recounted how one lamb found his way right into the book: "The lamb with long black ears which we saw in Palestine is our idea of just what a lamb should be. This particular lamb was found in the marketplace of Bethlehem when we were collecting material for the illustrations of *The Christ Child*."[5]

The Petershams traveled for three months in Palestine, countryside and town, to research customs and costumes for *The Christ Child*, as they had done for the earlier books set in France and Holland. "The farthest from home Miska and I have been is Jerusalem, with its high stone walls and gates leading into little narrow streets crowded with sheep and camels and donkeys and people—just like the people of the Bible stories." They spoke of this trip fondly—and often.[6]

Classic Old Testament Personages

The four *Stories From the Old Testament*, published seven years after *The Christ Child*, also relied on the original biblical text, this time to tell the stories of Joseph, Moses, Ruth and David. These tales were published by John C. Winston, with the four stories offered both as separate books and as a single compilation.[7] The color illustrations carry a non-reader from page to page, following along as someone reads the story—or perhaps can even tell the story in themselves, without the need for an adult reader.

Several years after *The Christ Child* was published, but prior to *Stories From the Old Testament*, a mother in Washington, D.C., wrote the Petershams with a complaint—and some not-so-faint praise:

> I feel that you stand preeminent in your field . . . I speak with some knowledge of the subject for I am the mother of four children, President of a school board, a lover of books in general, and I believe I see every new children's book that is published. . . . From my point of view and that of my children *The Ark of Father Noah and Mother Noah* has been your greatest triumph. I wished that in *The Christ Child* you might have told the story in your own words . . . I wish I might commission you to make the books I want my children to have, for instance, the story of Joseph and his Brethren—have you ever considered that?[8]

It is impossible to know whether the views of this woman played any part in the Petershams' decision to include Joseph in the Old Testament compilation, but Maud did keep her letter.

The Petershams' illustrations for *Moses* are a good example of how they researched their work—not only through travel, but also by visiting museums and consulting as many books and other sources as they could. One reviewer noted their "expert adaptation, slightly stylized, of Egyptian art, filled with authentic touches of ancient life yet presented with intimate quality usual to the authors' work."[9] Maud recounts in a handwritten note that Miska was the model for the drawings of Moses: "I will never forget Miska posing on the hottest days of August covered with his woolen Palestine coat, streams of water running down his face."[10]

The "Little New Testament"

The Petershams' *The Story of Jesus*, released in 1942, gathers verses from the Gospels (mostly Matthew and Luke) to tell the whole story of Jesus' life.[11] The book is organized so as to be helpful for someone encountering this text for the first time, with headings such as Birth and Childhood, Friends of Jesus, Stories That Jesus Told, Miracles, and Jesus' Death and Resurrection. Subtitled *A Little New Testament*, the small book is mainly text, unlike the earlier Bible stories, which rely heavily on illustrations to carry the story.

The only book that Maud produced alone was *The Shepherd Psalm*, published in 1962, two years after Miska's death. It is an illuminated text of the Twenty-third Psalm ("The Lord Is My Shepherd" is a common English translation of the first line), often called the "Psalm of Consolation." It also serves as a traditional biblical commentary, even akin to the Jewish midrash tradition, a form of detailed explication that fills in details of narrative and setting. Each spread includes a verse of the Psalm, a full-page illustration and Maud's own description of the period in which it was written—the role of shepherds, the importance of

water, how people lived in that time and place. Her sensitive introduction tells us a little about King David—what he might have been thinking at the time when he wrote the Psalm.

Scriptural Literacy: An Ear for the Spiritual

Both Maud and Miska brought to their work a childhood grounding in religion that was typical of nineteenth-century Western culture. Miska was baptized in the Catholic Church, but people who knew him report that he did not attend Mass or talk about religion very much.[12] Maud did not belong to a congregation as an adult, but her father was a Baptist minister and she had spent summers with her Quaker grandfather. Knowledge of the Bible and religious practice were woven into the fabric of household life.

While Quakers and Baptists appear to have little in common today, when Maud was growing up there were many similarities between the two. The Quaker scholar Howard H. Brinton characterizes the Baptists as one notch away from Quakers on a continuum from the highly structured Catholicism to the deeply personal religion of Quakerism.[13] Both sects place an emphasis on the personal nature of one's relationship to deity, essentially unmediated by a priesthood or set of rules. Both Baptists and Quakers encouraged daily Bible reading and the kind of scriptural knowledge that comes with constant exposure from earliest childhood.

Maud's close acquaintanceship with scripture is indicated in a handwritten list headed, "Brave Children of the Bible," perhaps an early plan for a book. Next to each name she has put

THIS BOOK IS FOR YOU

NOT FOR YOUR MOTHER
NOT FOR YOUR FATHER
JUST FOR YOU

The dedication page from *The Ark of Father Noah and Mother Noah*—
"This book is for you, not for your mother, not for your father, just
for you"—illustrates a recurring theme in the Petershams' work: the
absence of parents along with an emphasis on the individuality of
each child. In their early picture books (chapter 3) no adults accom-
pany the youngsters on their wild adventures, and in their later books
(chapter 7) this sense of encouraging independence is also apparent.

chapter and verse notations. The list includes
many familiar characters—Isaac and Joseph,
Moses and David—but also Jephtha's Daughter
(Judges: 11:34-40) and Little Friend of Elijah
(Kings: 17). Such a book was never published,
but this kernel of an idea suggests Maud's depth
of knowledge in the biblical field.

But one must not think that all of this reverence for the Bible meant that Maud and Miska
were grave and serious people. Maud loved to
recite a letter she received in 1938 from an eight-
year-old fan: "Dear Mr. and Mrs. Petersham, I am
reading the *Stories From the Old Testament*. I like
the pictures of the animals. I love the holy pictures very much too. My favorite story is about
Moses. Would you write me a book just about
boys and girls having fun?" At the top of the page,
Maud wrote, "This letter speaks for itself!"[14]

Important Books in This Chapter

The Ark of Father Noah and Mother Noah. Doubleday,
Doran, 1930

The Christ Child. Doubleday, 1931

Stories From the Old Testament. John C. Winston, 1938
The series compiles the following titles, also published
separately:

Joseph and His Brothers. John C. Winston, 1938
Moses. John C. Winston, 1938
David. John C. Winston, 1938
Ruth. John C. Winston, 1938

The Story of Jesus: A Little New Testament. Macmillan,
1942

The Shepherd's Psalm. Macmillan, 1962

The Ark of Father Noah and Mother Noah is a retelling of the flood story in the Book of Genesis, "as seen by Maud and Miska Petersham." They preserve the mythic quality of the original story but add human touches of humor and pathos. *The Ark* was a showcase for the Petershams' lively sense of color and design. Miska worked very closely with the printer Charles Stringer; together they delivered more than sixteen hues in these illustrations, using just six ink colors.

Della MacGregor, an influential figure in the world of children's librarianship, was ecstatic about her advance copy of *The Ark of Father Noah and Mother Noah*. Doubleday, Doran, as part of its marketing efforts, sent out material before books were published. Librarians were—and still are—among the most important market-makers for children's books; publishers quite rightfully treat them with respect.

Yesterday brought the dummy for NOAH'S ARK. . . . The Petershams have covered themselves with glory! They always do with their illustrations, and now they have done it in the text as well! . . . It is so refreshing to have such a delightful book, made with the real interest of the child at heart as well as the real understanding of the child's point of view. — Della MacGregor, head of Children's Services, St. Paul Public Library, and professor of Library Science

Poor Father Noah! He had made a mistake. The door of the Ark was a little too small for some of the very, very large animals to go in.

It was raining harder now and there was no time nor chance to enlarge the opening.

So these great big animals, the very biggest, had to be left out of the Ark.

This is a rather poignant explanation of why woolly mammoths and dinosaurs no longer walk the earth. The Petershams are clear-sighted about the fact that people make mistakes, including themselves. Here they dramatically demonstrate that grown-ups, even biblical ones, are not infallible—and that mistakes can have grave consequences.

Mother Noah told the animals every story that she ever knew.

The day came when she couldn't think of another one.

Then Father Noah took his turn.

Life was claustrophobic and boring on the Ark, but Mother Noah and Father Noah had a store of strategies to keep the passengers cheerful and to distract them from their plight. Once again, the Petershams leaven difficult material with gentle humor.

That stopped the parade.

"Each day Father Noah planned a parade around the Ark to keep their spirits up." But one day, bored to distraction, the elephants at the head of the parade stopped dead, with repercussions all the way to the back. It is easy for the reader to identify with the boredom of one rainy day after another, and refreshing to be able to laugh at incidents such as this. — From *The Ark of Father Noah and Mother Noah*

In *The Christ Child*, the Petershams selected the text directly from the King James version of Matthew and Luke, rather than retell it for children. Their colorful illustrations—filled with drama, humor and detail—carry the nativity story for the youngster, even when the language is hard to understand.

We spent three months in Palestine, and there all the Bible stories I learned as a child became a truth. When we stood in the marketplace in Jerusalem, the Bible figures were right there in front of us just as they might have been 2,000 years ago. The camels, and the shepherds with their long-eared sheep passed like a parade in front of us. — Maud, in a 1947 radio interview

Maud Cadman formed a shipboard friendship with the Petershams on the way to Jerusalem and other parts of what was then Palestine during their travels in preparation for *The Christ Child*.

Llandudno (Wales), December 4, 1931
Dear Mrs. Petersham,

I am simply delighted with your book, "The Christ Child." . . .

It really was charming of you to remember to send me a copy and to have autographed it. I shall always treasure it. It will always serve to remind me of the pleasure of your society on the "Pierre Loti" and on the return journey when we happened again to be traveling on the same boat.

I hope your young son is very well. He is lucky in being the possessor of such talented parents. — Maud Cadman

This illustration from *The Christ Child* was also used on the cover, and for many readers the image remained in their minds as an iconic manger scene.

When we were asked to make The Christ Child, *I said we couldn't possibly do it unless we saw what the Bible Country was actually like. It worked out that we spent three months wandering in and about Jerusalem and from Bethlehem to the Sea of Galilee. We brought back from Palestine costumes, which have helped us with our other Bible Stories . . . Getting material from the real thing rather than from photographs has been one of our great pleasures.* — Maud, in a handwritten note

MOSES

FROM THE STORY TOLD IN THE OLD TESTAMENT

Title page from *Moses*. This was one of four stories from the Old Testament that were published by John C. Winston in 1938 both as separate books and as a collection in a single volume.

The illustrations for . . . Moses are especially pleasing in their expert adaptation, slightly stylized, of Egyptian art, filled with authentic touches of ancient life yet presented with the intimate quality usual to the authors' work. — Ulster County (N.Y.) News

Maud describes hard and physically demanding work on the Bible illustrations for Moses during a summer near Gananoque, Ontario, but she is able to step back and joke about how they must have looked to people on passing boats. This kind of perspective often surfaced when Maud and Miska spoke about themselves, demonstrating that the words "humor" and "humility" have the same root—and the Petershams had both qualities in full measure:

I will never forget Miska posing on the hottest days of August covered with his woolen Palestine coat . . . as Moses—he stood up on a table with the tablets in his hands over and over again—dying on his feet—because I just couldn't get the right feeling in the pose I was trying to sketch. We were working that summer on an island in the Saint Lawrence River and it was like living in a gold fish bowl—as Miska suffered and I suffered trying to get what I wanted—as boats went round and round the island—trying to figure out what these crazy artists could be doing. — Maud, in a handwritten note

Illustration of the death of Moses, with a gentle rewriting of the account recorded in the Book of Deuteronomy:

And God said, "this is the land which I promised. I have caused you to see it with your eyes, but you shall not go over into it." So Moses, the servant of the Lord, died there on the mountain top. There was never after a prophet in the land of Israel like Moses, whom God knew face to face.

For an indication of the Petershams' respect for scripture throughout these tales, compare their work above to the text in the King James Bible:

And the LORD said unto him, This is the land which I sware unto Abraham, unto Isaac, and unto Jacob, saying, I will give it unto thy seed: I have caused thee to see it with thine eyes, but thou shalt not go over thither . . . And there arose not a prophet since in Israel like unto Moses, whom the LORD knew face to face . . . — Deuteronomy 34:4 and 34:10

Title page from *Ruth*.

Our trip to Palestine helped us with the pictures for this book. From the stormy day we left the steamer and were rowed between the black rocks of Jaffa to the shore, each day was exciting . . . One day we walked from Jerusalem to Bethlehem, and it was on this walk that we saw and heard the singing camel. . . . Even the short time we had in Palestine gave us a little understanding of the country and of the people. And we have tried to put this feeling into the pictures of these Stories From the Old Testament. *We have drawn and painted the pictures hoping they may make the stories of Joseph, of Moses, of Ruth and of David, more real for you.* — Maud, in *Young Wings: The Magazine of the Boys' and Girls' Own Book Club*

Illustration from *Ruth*: gleaning (gathering grain left by reapers). The stories in the Bible were part of Maud's consciousness, and she wrote about how, with Miska, she came to create these illustrated Bible stories:

As a child, I had all kinds of Bible Story books with pictures good and bad. But there was only one I really loved and felt satisfied with. Then one day my father, who was a minister, took this special book to a little child—a child who was very sick in the hospital. The book was lost. Father promised to get me another like it, but we were never able to find another copy. So perhaps in making the book we have just finished there was a feeling of making a book which would take the place of the one I lost when I was a child. — Maud, in *Young Wings: The Magazine of the Boys' and Girls' Own Book Club*

JOSEPH AND HIS BROTHERS

FROM THE STORY TOLD IN THE BOOK OF GENESIS

Title page from *Joseph and His Brothers* (1938). A *New York Herald Tribune* reviewer compared Maud and Miska's art to that of James Tissot (1836–1902), a French-born artist whose biblical illustrations were popular in Great Britain and North America and would have been known to the Petershams.

These thoroughly satisfactory pictures . . . though bright, they are mellow and glowing rather than striking. That quality is left to the vigor of their designs; all their scenes are at great moments and in none is it possible to forget these are people of sinew and purpose, men who make destiny. They are more like the wiry tribesman of Tissot's paintings than those in the plump Teutonic pictures of so many family Bibles; they have a wild charm. — *New York Herald Tribune*

DAVID

FROM THE STORY TOLD IN THE FIRST BOOK OF SAMUEL AND THE FIRST BOOK OF KINGS

OPPOSITE Title page from *David*, the last of the four Old Testament stories, published in 1938.

THE SHEPHERD BOY

WHILE Saul was king of Israel, a man called Jesse lived with his sons in Bethlehem. Among the sons there was one whom God had chosen to be the next king.

Preliminary sketch for an illustration of David as a young shepherd (see next plate). The Petershams' young son, Miki, was often pressed into service as a model.

These books mean everything to us because they have in them a little of [the] most precious things we own. . . . Our child, 12 years old when these pictures were made (now he is no longer a boy and no use to us for posing) had the boyish, almost-man body just right for David when he met Goliath . . . — Maud, in a handwritten note

Illustration from *David*, showing the sketch in the previous plate fully realized.

The John C. Winston Company are fortunate, indeed, to have the authors with their mastery of the process, handle all the complicated mechanics of six color reproduction. Under less skillful hands it would be impossible to catch the subtleties of the original plates. Perhaps that is one of the main reasons for the strong personal charm of all [the Petershams'] work, for from the moment when the first idea comes until the book is actually in the press, the authors have guided and molded it into its final form. — Helen H. Shotwell, *Ulster County (N.Y.) News*

Frontispiece from *The Story of Jesus*, the Petershams' illustrated story of the life and works of Jesus and the Apostles. As with the Old Testament stories, here they were respectful of the King James text.

Called "a little New Testament," the text of this companion of childhood is that of the King James Version printed "like a story" and altered only to tell without repetition the story of Jesus. It goes directly to children as young as eight, while its many beautiful pictures, illuminating the text for those who can read it, will introduce incidents and bring out its message to children yet too young for reading . . . These are the work of artists who know the land, the people, and the Book and have proved their power to inspire in children the reverent affection that these illustrations express. — Review in the *New York Herald Tribune*

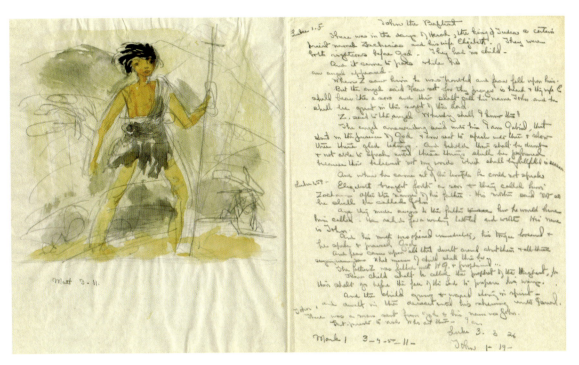

Dummy spread for *The Story of Jesus*, written in Maud's hand, with specific references to chapter and verse in the New Testament. It is likely that Maud did not have to look up the sources—she would have known these stories in some detail after growing up in her father's parsonage and spending long hours in church and in Bible study.

The Shepherd Psalm

Maud Petersham

Cover of *The Shepherd Psalm*, published in 1962. This was the only book that Maud finished after Miska's death in 1960. Each two-page spread includes one verse of the familiar "Lord Is My Shepherd" psalm, an illustration, and Maud's own explanation of the significance of such things as shepherds and green pastures to the desert pastoral nomads who created the Psalms.

With courage clear and faith triumphant over fear, Maud Petersham presents this beautiful
Bible Psalm. A Caldecott winner along with her late husband, her wondrous work continues
to bless child and adult alike.   — *Marin Independent Journal*

In *The Shepherd Psalm* Maud conveys the importance of shepherds in the Middle East during biblical times, and the challenges of keeping a flock safe in the arid wilderness.

The Shepherd Psalm by Maud Petersham is a must! Beauty, clarity, exquisite design, and helpful notes are on every page of this lovely book. . . . One verse of the twenty-third psalm appears on each page . . . along with excellent notes describing the shepherd's daily life in Judea. On each facing page is a full illustration in strong lines and soft pastels. It is a beautiful portrayal of both the psalm itself and its concept of the Lord as a faithful shepherd. — Winston-Salem (N.C.) Journal

CHAPTER 5

The World Around Us

Learning, Science and Technology

This series set a new standard in nonfiction for children.[1]

The Petershams' vivid pictures of past and present life represented reality to a generation of American children. . . .

— Sarah L. Rueter in Bader's *American Picturebooks* [2]

Sandwiched between *Get-A-Way and Háry János* and *Miki and Mary* were four non-fiction titles the Petershams took on for John C. Winston. *The Story Book of Things We Use*, released in 1933, was also published as four separate books: *The Story Book of Houses* and a story book each on *Clothes*, *Food* and *Transportation*. Over a period of five years they produced twenty individual titles, published both separately and as five four-part compilations.

Specialists in children's literature agree that with these books the Petershams were once again pioneers. The books are chockablock with authoritative information, presented in an engaging and accessible way, drawing the reader in through vibrant pictures, beautiful color, a sense of action and applicability to one's own life.[3]

Taken together, these books represent a monumental amount of painstaking work, even if assessed only in numbers: Each of the twenty titles is a thirty-two-page book with a picture on every page, as often as not in full color. That is six hundred and forty pages and perhaps three hundred color illustrations to be designed and executed. This in addition to researching and writing on just about every subject imaginable, from cave dwellings—and cave paintings—to modern oil exploration, air travel and agribusiness.

A Worldview Brimming With Curiosity and Faith in Progress

In an interview, Miska told a group of children that he and Maud were inspired by Miki, who was ten years old when the first of these nonfiction books was published. "When our own little boy . . . used to come into our bed . . . we ran out of fairy tales and all the other stories so we started to tell him about factual things . . . and go to the fields and woods and

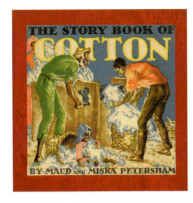
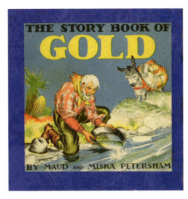
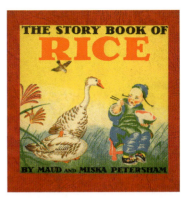
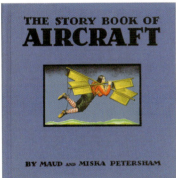
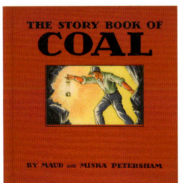
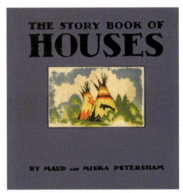
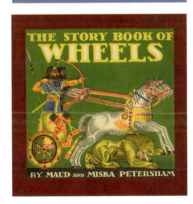
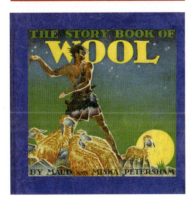
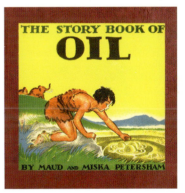

This image shows nine of the twenty individual titles in the Petershams' *The Story Book of . . .* series, produced in just seven years, from 1933 to 1939. The square format and interior layout are consistent across the entire series.

The lavishly colored, detailed illustrations for the Petershams' series of informational storybooks . . . set a new standard in nonfiction for children. — Sarah L. Rueter, in *Children's Books and Their Creators*

think about early man, tasting things, roasting things. So many things were discovered accidentally."[4] One can picture the boisterous child of eight or nine jumping on the bed of his storytelling parents, asking question after question—and ultimately sending them to the encyclopedia and the library to learn more about the many subjects of his quizzing.

The sheer range of subject matter is as wide as a child's curiosity. Each of these books communicates a sense of joy in the very act of learning about the world in which we live. A belief in the goodness of human progress and technology undergirds all of these titles, and there is a sense of gradual change in such disparate matters as air transport or farming or the cultivation of silkworms. But alongside the admiration for progress, there is a wide net of diversity across both time and space. The child who discovers fire with his Neolithic cave-dwelling family is just as much a little boy as Miki was in 1933; the detailed illustrations pull us in, making us want to stay a while. The children's literature scholar Barbara Bader says it so well: "In Petershamland remote past and remote present are indistinguishable—and almost always there are children, enviable children, to second the invitation."[5]

While their technical information was current, they also used ancient sources such as Assyrian, Greek, Chinese, Japanese, Egyptian and medieval paintings. "Their scope and purpose were novel."[6] Although the technical information may be dated—consider what has transpired since 1938 in transportation, or in housing, or, for that matter, in our approach to history—there is much here that is still of interest and value in the integration of visual and verbal material.

Filling an Empty Niche

"I like the *Story Book of Coal* because it helped me in my geography lesson," a youngster from Iowa wrote to Maud and Miska. "It was interesting, too. I liked the pictures very much. I had to make a report on this book. It was easy because of the pictures which helped me to explain what I said."[7] These books served as kind of pre-encyclopedias. But they offer more than simple information. Each is populated by children—and by little stories, whether told in the colorful, detailed pictures or in the text. Many elementary-school teachers and librarians used these as a first exposure to research, although the books also make good fodder for reading aloud or reading to oneself. Miska expressed the seriousness with which they took this project: "In these books we made up our minds there would not be a single page of text or a single illustration which would not be of vital interest to a child." But then his sense of humor twinkled when he was asked how they divided their work on the series: "Mrs. Petersham did most of the writing and I did the criticizing."[8]

Clever Marketing

John C. Winston was quite imaginative in marketing these titles. Maud's sister Winifred was the executive secretary at St. Agnes School in Virginia, and she sent Maud a short but effusive publicity flier that she had received at school, writing a note across the top: "Thought you might be interested in seeing what kind of a selling job Winston was doing."[9] In addition to vigorous school and library marketing, Winston sent each of the titles to the appropriate manufacturing or professional association. The President of the Southern Rice Sales Company responded with a stiff and formal letter expressing a cheerful sentiment—as though a bit of the visual exuberance had rubbed off on him: "There have been commercial thrills of one kind or another during my career in the Rice Industry, but never have I experienced anything resembling an aesthetic sensation until the receipt of your charming book. I intend to afford the same pleasure to a number of my business acquaintances and friends. It is delightful and I very much appreciate your thoughtfulness in sending a copy to me."[10] Winston had similar success with the Celanese corporation in promoting the Petershams' *Rayon* book.

Planning was under way for additional titles in this series—the archives include some notes and reworked lists as well as memos from the publisher about other possible titles: writing or the alphabet, printing or books, money or communications. Maud's handwritten notes in response are an interesting window onto her expansive way of thinking. Under the heading "The Story Book of Money," she has jotted down a list: "exchange or barter; things used as money—salt, cattle, shells, beads, beaver skins, tobacco, coal, leather, coins as money—Egypt, Libya; leather; metals are easy to handle, don't change with time, can be divided into units." Under "Inter-Communication" she has written, "the Story Book of Carrying Mail—messengers to airplanes; The Story Book of Money; Barter to Banks; the Story Book of Communication—Signaling to Wireless; Writing—Picture Writing to Modern Books . . ."[11]

This series had wide circulation, including Japanese and Spanish editions of many titles.

The Story Book of the Earth's Treasures was chosen as one of just twenty-eight children's books making up a gift to the White House Library from the American Booksellers Association. The titles were selected from among all those published in the United States over a four-year period. *Treasures* is in good company on this list: The other titles include Emily Dickinson's *Poems for Youth* and Ingri and Edgar Parin D'Aulaire's *George Washington* and *Caddie Woodlawn*.[12]

In its review of *The Story Book of Things We Wear*, the last book in the series, the *New York Times* might have been referring to all of Maud and Miska's work:

> The Petershams know how to invest the affairs of everyday with romance. They see things largely and against a historical background. Cotton and wool and silk are important clothing materials of today and modern spinning and weaving are fully and carefully described, but these author-illustrators show, too, the sheepfolds and shepherds of early times, ancient Egyptians in their woven garments, English weavers of the Middle ages, and a maid of ancient Greece spinning wool, as they found her on a Greek vase of the fifth century B.C.[13]

Important Books in This Chapter

The Story Book of . . .
Things We Use. John C. Winston, 1933. Individual titles were *Houses*, *Clothes*, *Food*, *Transportation*.
Wheels, Ships, Trains, Aircraft. John C. Winston, 1935. These four were also published as individual titles.
The Earth's Treasures. John C. Winston, 1935. Individual titles were *Gold*, *Coal*, *Oil*, *Iron and Steel*.
Foods From the Field. John C. Winston, 1936. Individual titles were *Wheat*, *Corn*, *Rice*, *Sugar*.
Things We Wear. John C. Winston, 1939. Individual titles were *Wool*, *Cotton*, *Silk*, *Rayon*.

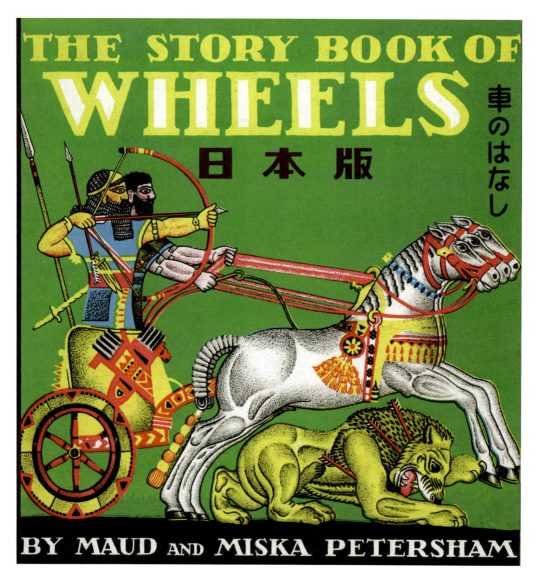

The Story Book of . . . nonfiction series was translated into many languages. Here is the cover of the Japanese edition of The Story Book of Wheels.

Interior spread from the Japanese edition of *The Story Book of Wheels.*

The Story Book of . . . series included:

Political history, ethnology, economics, technology, oddity—the range is enormous, hardly less than the story of man's works reconceived for children and reconstituted in pictures. — Sarah L. Rueter in Bader's *American Picturebooks*

Detail from "The Peasant House" in *The Story Book of Houses*.

In Petershamland remote past and remote present are indistinguishable. — Barbara Bader, *American Picturebooks*

Detail from "The Pueblo" in *The Story Book of Houses*. Typical of the books in this series, each picture provides the characters and setting for a little story of its own.

Detail from "The Lake Dwellers," in *The Story Book of Houses.*

Long years ago these houses were all covered by the waters of the lake or the swamp in which they were built. Nobody dreamed that they were there. Then there came a very dry summer in Switzerland. There was no rain for weeks. The lake water became lower and lower, and pretty soon someone saw poles sticking up, and a rough platform. There were the lake dwellings of long ago. — Text on the page with this illustration, from *The Story Book of Houses*

Canary birds are a part of the equipment of every mine. When there is danger of deadly gas being in the mine, the little bird in its cage is taken down and watched very carefully. Long before the men can smell the gas or detect its presence, the bird is overcome and the warning given. The canaries are revived in the fresh air.

How often do we use the phrase "canary in the coal mine" to mean first alarm, first sign of trouble? This illustration and its accompanying text, from *The Story Book of Coal*, remind us graphically of the source of this common saying. This is from the compilation *The Story Book of the Earth's Treasures*, along with *Gold*, *Oil*, and *Iron and Steel*.

Illustration from *The Story Book of Oil*. Here, the Petershams' careful research is again in evidence. The accompanying text resonates today, nearly eight decades on.

. . . under the sand, the British lay a thousand miles of pipe line. This buried pipe transports oil from the rich fields of Iraq, the home of the Arabs, to ports on the Mediterranean Sea. From these ports tank steamers carry the oil across the oceans. — Text on the page with this illustration from *The Story Book of Oil*

A clever presentation of complex information, showing how oil gets from deep wells to gas tanks, this illustration from *The Story Book of Oil* shows the Petershams' skill in presenting technical information.

Oil has become more and more necessary to everyone. . . . Now, if the supply of oil were cut off, our manner of living would change completely until something to take its place was found. — Text on the last page of *The Story Book of Oil*

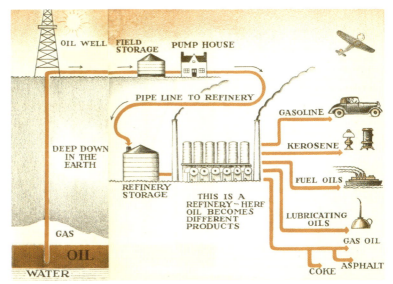

Detail from *The Story Book of Rice*, one of the four *Foods From the Field* books, along with *Wheat*, *Corn* and *Sugar*.

The sketch on the left is from a dummy for *The Story Book of Food*, 1933. An editorial memorandum listed a number of small changes to the dummy, including this note: "p. 10, make sure that the reaper is up-to-date." The image on the right is the finished illustration from the printed book for the same spread. The text remained unchanged from the dummy to the final printing.

This picture shows one of our great wheat fields. The man is cutting the wheat with a large machine. He can raise a great deal of wheat by using machines to plant the wheat and to cut it. — Text on the page opposite this illustration from *The Story Book of Food*

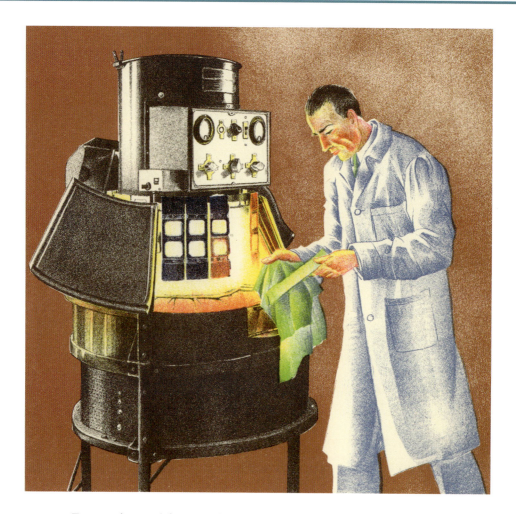

Testing color in a fad-o-meter, from *The Story Book of Rayon*. The letter below, from a leading U.S. rayon manufacturer, illustrates the multi-channel marketing strategy used by the publisher, John C. Winston. These storybooks were sent to the appropriate industry leaders and trade associations as well as to institutions representing the traditional markets for children's books.

Dear Mr. & Mrs. Petersham,

I have just received in this morning's mail a copy of your story book on rayon, and hasten to congratulate you on this splendid little book with its beautiful illustrations and concise, easily understandable text.

I have written to our friend, Jack Frazier, and ordered a dozen for our company to be used as Christmas presents.

I believe that most all rayon companies would be interested in acquiring a number of these useful little books.

When you are in NY again, please let me hear from you. — Arthur L. Erlanger, Erlanger Mills (in New York City)

Detail from *The Story Book of Wool*. The shepherd with his flock is a familiar image in the Petershams' work.

Another kind of shepherd, also from *The Story Book of Wool*. The Rocky Mountain shepherd wagons, introduced by Basque immigrants in the nineteenth century, are in use to this day.

The high Rockies in the United States are ideal summer pastures for millions of sheep. The herder leads a lonely life. Often for months on end his only home is far out on the range in a covered wagon. Here he sleeps and builds his fire and cooks his food, his sheep asleep around him. His sheep and his dog are his only companions. — Text on the page with this illustration, from *The Story Book of Wool*

CHAPTER 6

Appreciating America
American Folklore and History

*We are trying to put before the children of this country those
things which are theirs for the taking.*

— Miska Petersham, from his 1946 acceptance speech
upon receiving the Caldecott Medal for *The
Rooster Crows: A Book of American Rhymes and Jingles* [1]

During the 1940s and 1950s the Petershams focused their creative efforts on their country, bringing out six books with specifically American themes and subject matter under the editorship of Doris Patee at Macmillan. During the 1950s these titles were marketed as a series, "This Is America," and distributed internationally by the Agency for International Development. The titles were quite varied—nonfiction and history; folklore and fiction—but the Petershams' characteristic care and precision show on every meticulously researched and illustrated page.

The Petershams were rooted in America in two very different ways. Miska, who arrived at Ellis Island in 1912, had the fervor of the new immigrant, the first-generation naturalized citizen; Maud reflected the quiet pride of a *Mayflower* descendant whose American roots were so much a part of her that she spoke little about them. Their combined sensibilities communicated a deep and multifaceted appreciation of America—a patriotism quite free of isolationism and xenophobia. Their approach in these six books helped to form the perceptions and assumptions about America and its history held by the postwar generation of youngsters.

Children's Book Week Posters: Tracing the Arc of America's Self-Image

The Petershams' three national Children's Book Week posters reflect the nation's changing attitudes toward itself and other countries. The first, in 1931, was typical of their work of that time, conveying an international theme with the header, "Round the World Book Fair." In 1940, with World War II raging in Europe, the poster shows children in military-like formation, holding books as if in salute, over the slogan "Good Books, Good Friends." In 1946, the terrible conflict just over and in a spirit of fence-mending

A is for AMERICA
The land I love

Illustration from *An American ABC*, chosen as a Caldecott Honor book in 1942. The Petershams used the alphabet book to present snippets of American history and mythology. Here, the child is safely asleep, his model airplane beside him—under the watchful eye of the American eagle, a rather fierce nanny.

In 1941. . . we welcomed An American ABC *with its spirited interpretations of The Liberty Bell, The Declaration of Independence, the Mayflower, Yankee Doodle, and other symbols of our national life. The artists offered it as an expression of their own vital creed.* — Irene Smith Green, *Horn Book Magazine*, April 1946

and relationship-building, "Books Are Bridges" served as a counterpoint to Bennett Cerf's wartime radio show, *Books Are Bullets.*[2]

Reflections of a National Mood

From the start, the "America" books struck a chord: *An American ABC*, named a Caldecott Honor book, was published in 1941, months before Pearl Harbor and America's entry into the war. As one of the book's reviewers put it, referring to the discomfort Americans were feeling about the war, "In 1941 we were more aware of America than we had been since 1917."[3] The American Library Association began honoring illustrators for distinguished work in 1938, choosing one Medalist and a handful of Honor books. When the Petershams were first so recognized, the Caldecott was just in its fourth year. The 1941 winner had been Robert Lawson's *They Were Strong and Good*, a tribute to the author-illustrator's ancestors and a celebration of that elusive thing, "character." (One is reminded of Maud's gentle voice in Lawson's Preface about his forbears: "None of them were great or famous, but they were strong and good.") *An American ABC* takes the reader through the alphabet with illustrated vignettes, from "A Is for America, the Land That I Love" to "Z Is for Zeal, An American Trait." Historical subjects include Christopher Columbus, George Washington and the *Mayflower*, while cultural and conceptual references include "N, National Anthem, The Star Spangled Banner" and "W, White House, and the city of Washington, the home of our government." Several vignettes are particularly notable given the disparate backgrounds of Maud and Miska: "M is for Mayflower, the

Pilgrim's Ship," "Q is for Quakers, and Quakers are Friends," and "E is for Emigrants, People who leave their own land to make new homes in another land. . . . People from all over the world are still coming to our shores. Good emigrants make true Americans."

The influential critic May Lamberton Becker praised the book mightily: "Patriotism of the kind that counts is not only the keynote but the melodic scheme of this beautiful picture book with accompanying text . . . As authors and as artists the Petershams have set out to show children something about the America into which they were born or to which they have come, awakening thereby a sense that there is something beautiful and glorious about America, something worth living for"[4]—perhaps something like "F is for Freedom, that precious thing for which America Stands."

It was not only the critics who enjoyed the *ABC*. A teacher wrote an exuberant note on behalf of "The Boys and Girls of Ogden Public Schools, Ogden, Utah" about a multimedia, school-wide celebration, all based on the Petershams' book:

In all our mortal days we have never enjoyed a book so much as your American ABC. . . . it has gone through the school like wildfire. A regular fever of patriotism has broken out in the Pingree School. All of us are getting those nice little tingly feelings running up and down our spines . . . Now we are making your book of ABCs into a beautiful pageant for Book Week and American Education Week . . . for our parents and all the children in our school and even in some of the other schools. . . . We do wish you might see how everyone is ABCing. . . . We are ABCing in the auditorium with the pageant, in the home rooms we are making original ABCs, in the physical education room some of the children have made dances to the different rhythms of the ABCs— and some very fine health poems. . . . Our supervisor Miss McCracken and our principal Mr. Barney said there was more history in that little book than they ever learned.[5]

It is not surprising to learn that Maud took great pains to save this letter.

Rooster Wins a Medal

The Rooster Crows: A Book of American Rhymes and Jingles, published in 1945, is one of the few Petersham titles still in print, and it is so because it won the 1946 Caldecott Medal, the most prestigious award an American children's illustrator can receive. The book is a compilation of traditional rhymes and jingles, illustrated with humor and drama. Maud poignantly described writing and illustrating *The Rooster Crows* as an escape from wartime worries, as their son was active in the Air Corps in the Pacific:

> One night while trying to forget the eleven o'clock news which we had just heard, and while trying to put away the worry that so many weeks had passed since we had heard from our child, I played a childish game with myself. Instead of counting sheep I tried to recall the foolish little rhymes and jingles I had not thought of for so many years. In the morning I went to my desk and wrote them down and then naturally they had to have illustrations. It was purely an escape move on our part but while we were working on those pictures we found we could live in a little world which was decidedly more sane than the real world was at that moment.[6]

Caldecott Medalists are celebrated at a dinner given at the American Library Association's annual conference, with much pomp and circumstance and an obligatory acceptance speech. Artists take these speeches seriously; Maud and Miska each worked through several drafts. Miska recounted his first months in America: "This friendly, open country was amazing and unbelievable to me. If I could not make myself understood right away, people would listen and help me. . . . In six months I was working. I had an apartment. . . . I owned a new suit of clothes from Wanamaker's and a pair of American-made shoes that all Europeans longed for, and I had extra money in my pocket for a glass of beer, which was presented with a roast-beef sandwich."[7]

And Maud, with characteristic humility, related how a reader wrote and alerted them to an error: "In the 'Bye Baby Bunting' picture, . . . Mother's gone to milk a cow, but alas our critic tells us Mother is sitting on the wrong side of the cow and at the wrong end of her anatomy. I can't claim to having ever achieved the art of milking, but I have seen cows—and something, I admit, is wrong with that picture."[8] Always ready to poke fun at herself and own up to the couple's mistakes, here Maud is telling the august gathering at the American Library Association that there is a flawed illustration in a book that has just won the Caldecott for the most distinguished illustrated book for children!

The awarding of a Caldecott Medal invites review, celebration and heaps of praise for the winning title. Some of the most comprehensive information about Maud and Miska comes from press surrounding the award, as well as from reviews in *Horn Book Magazine*, *Library Journal* and *Publishers Weekly*. The Medal has also secured the Petershams a place in encyclopedic works on the history of American children's literature.

Within twenty years of the book's publication, the reputation of *Rooster*, and by extension the Petershams, became tarnished. Two illustrations that were judged demeaning racial stereotypes were removed from the book in 1964 and in all subsequent printings. But this did not stop the critics. Throughout American society, the 1960s brought a new awareness of the racism that was so deeply embedded in the culture. Emblematic of this trend was "The All-White World of Children's Books," an article by a noted educator and champion of children's literature, in which she highlighted the general absence of Black characters in kids' books and, worse, pointed out that where Black characters were portrayed they were "the embodiments of unfortunate racial stereotypes."[9] She cited earlier editions of *The Rooster Crows* in particular for demeaning depictions of Black children, until, as Leonard S. Marcus put it, "after eighteen years enough complaints had been received to convince the publisher that the book would be improved by deleting the offending illustrations."[10]

The original edition of *Rooster* remained in library collections, of course, and Macmillan continued to field complaints and queries. Susan Carr Hirschman, a new member of the editorial staff at Macmillan (and soon to succeed Doris Patee as head of the department), wrote a gentle letter to Maud in 1966:

> How lovely to be writing to you again! This time it is with a rather strange question, and if you can't answer it, don't worry. . . . The Coordinator for Children's Services of the Westchester Public Library asked me yesterday if I could tell her the origins of the two Negro dialect verses in the unrevised edition of THE ROOSTER CROWS. Do you know where you found them? If you can tell me I will pass the information along to her. And if you don't remember, if you could just let me know I will tell her I can't find out.[11]

A follow-up note from Hirschman indicates that Maud had replied that she did not remember—and that is the last of any known correspondence on the matter.

Given what we know of how Maud and Miska lived their lives, honoring—even celebrating—differences among people of all kinds, it is tempting to argue that any stereotyping in their work was unconscious and not born of malice or prejudice. On the positive side, their books were less racially homogeneous than most in that generation—Asian and Black and Native American people did appear in many of their books; they were not invisible. On the negative side, many of those illustrations certainly used what are now considered demeaning conventions. What might have been standard fare in 1945 clearly appeared racist to the sensitized eye of the 1960s. Myra Cohn Livingston, writing the Petersham entry in *Twentieth Century Children's Writers*, stressed the positive with a preemptive strike:

> Certainly in dozens of books Miska Petersham showed his appreciation for America and Maud her religious background in a blending which showed respect for other cultures and races. . . . Although the Petersham texts may appear to be somewhat simplistic today, it is well to remember that their concern for multi-ethnic and racial consciousness made its first appearance in book form in 1929, many years before other authors and illustrators took into account this important aspect of books for the young reader.[12]

One reviewer's racism is another's multiculturalism.

Stamps: A Picture Window Onto American History

While enjoying the limelight as new Caldecott Medalists, Miska and Maud were hard at work on their next book, *America's Stamps: The Story of One Hundred Years of U.S. Postage Stamps.* The book combined their interest in American history and culture with one of Miska's greatest passions. Miska's stamp collection competed with golf and bridge for his spare time. The history of his adopted and beloved country was revealed in the study of postage stamps. "Working on *America's Stamps* gave me great pleasure; first because I love stamps, but still more important to me was the story of America back of each stamp—a story which we tried to put across in pictures and text." Maud echoed this sentiment: ". . . one cannot know their American stamps without being a better American."[13]

Their work was arduous—they carefully collected stamps, information and images for more than a year, working and reworking layout, artwork and text to ensure not only that the book would be an accurate introduction to the complex world of stamps, but also that it would be engaging and interesting. Maud wrote that she wanted to create the book she had been hoping to find: "I was in danger of becoming a 'stamp widow.' He spent so many long hours poring over his stamps with tweezers and microscope and catalogs in front him . . . I wanted to find out what it was that was so intriguing and exciting about the little squares of paper used as postage. I asked questions but got nowhere."[14] Even an excursion to the library was of no use, so they conceived a straightforward and comprehensive book to introduce a complex topic. *Stamps* combines technical information and precise imaging with stories. These are interleaved with dramatic color illustrations of, for example, a colonial seaport, a Pony Express stagecoach and an airplane soaring high over the ocean.

The *Philadelphia Inquirer* critic was effusive: "This is the sort of book to send any reviewer reaching for her A-1 List of Superlatives. But to write down words like 'beautiful' (the Petersham pictures are certainly that), 'fascinating' (you can open it anywhere and lose yourself in a story), and 'informative' (you don't know American history until you've seen this book) still does not sufficiently convey the delight and worth of this volume."[15] So, too, the *New York Herald Tribune*: "Once more the Petershams ring the bell—indeed, the Philatelic Foundation endorses it as 'presenting the attractions of stamp collecting to all ages.' But for young folks in particular, its brilliant color plates, beautifully reproduced stamps, and running narrative combining history with philately combine to present the subject as an intelligent beginner might ask to have it presented."[16]

Ben Franklin Illustrated

In the spirit and style of *The Rooster Crows*, the Petershams' 1951 tribute to Benjamin Franklin, *A Bird in the Hand: Sayings From Poor Richard's Almanack*, takes the form of lively full-page illustrations of two dozen or so of Franklin's most famous aphorisms. Some were serious: "A true friend is the best possession" and "Early to bed, early to rise." Some were funny: "If your head is wax, don't walk in the sun." A short biography of Franklin at the beginning, explaining how he came to publish *Poor Richard*, offers some historical context. Reviewers greeted the Petershams' book with good cheer: "The combination of the great Franklin and one of America's foremost author-illustrator teams results in a beautiful picture book. . . . These pictures will delight even the smallest child and the adult too will appreciate their robust humor so well suited to the homeliness of the text. The only problem with the book is that it is too short."[17]

Presidential Biography as Historical Narrative

In *Story of the Presidents of the United States of America*, American history marches forth through short biographies arranged chronologically. The entry for each president includes a common sobriquet, dates in office, dates of birth and death, and political party, as well as a brief narrative of the man's life with a focus on one or two events.

The Petershams do not write hagiography—nor do they mince words, describing the complexities and difficulties of the office in a way that youngsters might understand. Extracts from the concluding sentences of just a few entries may help to illustrate: "James Madison served eight troubled years as President." "When his duties as President ended, Monroe had very little money. . . . a feeble, stoop-shouldered man of seventy-three, he still wore the outmoded knee breeches, silver buckled shoes and three-cornered hat . . ." "Worn by political life and by old battle wounds, 'Old Hickory' [Andrew Jackson] retired . . . to the Hermitage." "The broken-hearted old general [Ulysses S. Grant] spent his last years in sickness and poverty writing his personal memoirs."

They also introduce complex matters in an even-handed way. On FDR and the New Deal:

"Franklin Roosevelt was one of our strongest, most powerful presidents. He had created a government with new responsibilities for the welfare of its people." On scandal in high places: "President Harding was friendly to a fault. He gave official posts to many of his friends, some of whom betrayed the solemn trust they had accepted . . . he had proved unfitted for the responsibilities of the high office he held."

Library Journal gave this work a glowing review, ensuring it a place on reference shelves throughout the nation: "Every school and children's library will want this for its attractive format, subject appeal, simplicity, and brevity . . . For children first, this [is a] splendid addition to the Petershams' *This is America* series. But it will have considerable appeal for parents . . . In the brief biographies of each president, the Petershams have accomplished the difficult task of telling something of the personality of each man and the facts of his life."[18]

The History of a Place Introducing the History of an Era

The Silver Mace: A Story of Williamsburg covers a wide swath of American history—from the early Jamestown of 1607 through the thriving plantation colony under royal governors to the dawn of the Revolution. By the 1950s Williamsburg, Virginia, had been restored and rebuilt and opened to the public as a living history museum. Funded largely by the Rockefeller family, this ambitious project helped to inaugurate a golden age of historic preservation in America that culminated in the Historic Preservation Act of 1966 and such institutions as the National Register of Historic Places. The underlying goal

is for ZEAL
An American trait

"Z for Zeal" and "F for Freedom" are the only two entries in *An American ABC* that are solely abstract concepts. Among the other entries are places ("W for White House and Washington," "V for Valley Forge") and people ("H for Henry Hudson," "G for George Washington"), all presented in a patriotic tone.

of the Williamsburg enterprise was to interpret American history by recreating, and allowing people to experience, the places where the early colonists and settlers walked and lived.

In their research for this book, Maud and Miska visited Williamsburg for an extended period, filling a sketchbook with notes and details on each of the buildings whose rendering would end up among the illustrations in *The Silver Mace.*

Reviewers appreciated the fact that great sweeps of history could be addressed using the device of place: "This charming book is a model of its kind. . . . A lot of history had to be compressed within these slim covers, but the authors have selected well and trace salient points in a manner that will hold the interest of the young reader."[19]

In this series of six books, simply, and with engaging illustrations, the Petershams presented to children the iconic moments in American history, and many of the iconic personalities. The books reflect a shifting national mood—a refreshed patriotism born of war. But Miska and Maud are at the same time clear-eyed in presenting the darker moments. Throughout, and especially in the choices for the *ABC* and the Ben Franklin book, their own values—hard work, good humor, ever-expanding knowledge—leap off the page. Their undying belief in young people as the hope for the future lit up Maud's 1946 Children's Book Week speech in New York: "We think ourselves very fortunate because we don't have to work for the heartsick grown-ups of today, but we work for eager responsive children."[20]

Important Books in This Chapter

An American ABC. Macmillan, 1941 (1942 Caldecott Honor)
The Rooster Crows: A Book of American Rhymes and Jingles. Macmillan, 1945 (1946 Caldecott Medal)
America's Stamps. Macmillan, 1947
A Bird in the Hand: Sayings From Poor Richard's Almanack. Macmillan, 1951
Story of the Presidents of the United States of America. Macmillan, 1953
The Silver Mace: A Story of Williamsburg. Macmillan, 1956

is for EMIGRANTS
People who leave their own land to make
new homes in another land

Emigrants from all the different countries of the world journeyed to this new land.

Our great-great-grandfathers, our grandfathers, even perhaps our fathers, were all emigrants to America.

Some came to seek their fortunes. Many were unhappy in their own countries and came here to escape ways of living which had been forced upon them. They left their homes in the Old World and came to find homes in the New. They came to America because this country stood for Freedom.

People from all over the world are still coming to our shores. Good emigrants make true Americans.

ABOVE AND OPPOSITE "E is for Emigrants," is part of a two-page spread from *An American ABC*. This illustration is reminiscent of many from the period 1880 to 1915, when waves of Eastern Europeans came to the United States. Miska himself arrived on Ellis Island in 1912, having spent a week in steerage aboard RMS *Olympic*.

I told him my English was not very good but that I was hoping to improve it in America and was also hoping to make my living with art. Then he patted me on the back and assured me that in America I would have no trouble in earning my living with art, although it might take a little time to get acquainted with the new country. He shook hands and wished me good luck and happy days in America. And that was my entrance into this country. — Miska, in his Caldecott acceptance speech, published in *Horn Book Magazine*

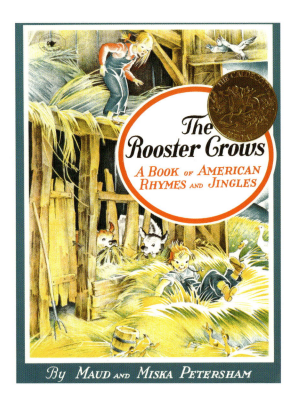

Cover from a late paperback edition of *The Rooster Crows*. Winner of the 1946 Caldecott Medal, *Rooster* is one of the few Petersham titles still in print. Maud rather poignantly described the writing and illustrating of this book as an escape from worry while their son was on active duty in the Pacific during World War II.

Illustration for "Bye Baby Bunting, Father's gone a-hunting," in *The Rooster Crows*. Always ready to admit mistakes, in her Caldecott acceptance speech Maud described a critical letter from a reader explaining that to milk a cow as shown in this picture is anatomically impossible.

"Old Mister Rabbit,
Your tail's mighty white."
"Yes, sir, Brother,
Gwin'ter take it out of sight."

This illustration is one of two that were taken out of later editions of *The Rooster Crows* on grounds of racial stereotyping, a reflection of the change in sensitivities between 1945, when the book was first published, and the 1960s.

Illustration from *The Rooster Crows*. This hayloft scene is reminiscent of the one in *Auntie*, thirteen years earlier. Maud had fond memories of hiding in haylofts during her childhood.

In the books we make I am happy when we can picture some of those wonderful things which American children can claim as their heritage. Working on An American ABC *meant a great deal to me aside from the making of the pictures. In* An American ABC *and in* The Rooster Crows *we have tried to put into the hands of children little snatches of history and stories that are rightfully theirs. And now we are working on a book of United States postage stamps, those small squares of paper commemorating events of which American children can be so proud.* — Miska, Caldecott acceptance speech, 1946

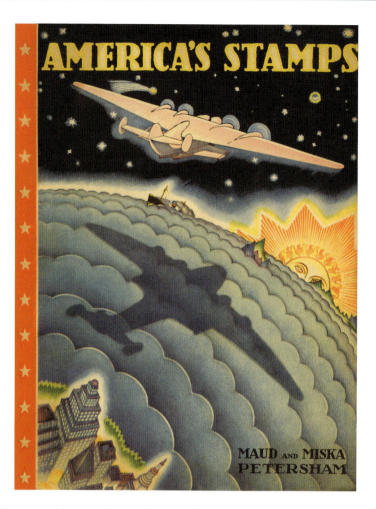

The cover of *America's Stamps*, showing a favorite Petersham image: round earth—there for any and all to traverse—rippling concentric waves, stylized sun, airplane and stars. Miska was an avid philatelist, poring for hours over his ever-growing collection. Maud researched this ambitious and comprehensive book partly in defense against becoming a "stamp widow," as she characterized it.

I will admit the details of this book practically floored us but I am now glad of the hard work we put into it. — Miska

. . . we decided to make a book, the kind we wanted for ourselves, showing all the American stamps in the order in which they were issued and telling a little of the story of the design or picture on the stamp itself and connecting it all together with the exciting story of American postal history, from the cocked-hat Continental post riders who followed Indian trails and the daring, courageous Pony Express boys armed with pistol and bowie knife, down through the lonely dangerous job of the pioneer night-flying pilots in their open-cockpit planes, to the clipper and great mail transport planes of today. — Maud

Dummy-to-book example. The top image is a mid-stage dummy spread for *America's Stamps*; the bottom image is the stagecoach illustration as finally printed. As a boy in Hungary, Miska was entranced by the American West, reading the adventure novels of the German writer Karl May—the European Zane Gray. Western images appear frequently in the Petershams' work.

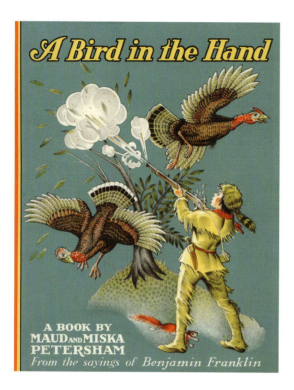

Cover for *A Bird in the Hand: Sayings From Poor Richard's Almanack*. The Petershams shared authorship with Benjamin Franklin and included a short biography of Franklin in this illustrated edition of some of his favorite sayings.

"If you would have a faithful servant . . . *serve yourself*," from *A Bird in the Hand*. An independent little girl climbs a tree and manages her harvest of apples with skill and agility. The cat-and-mouse drama at the base of the tree is typical of the tiny unspoken stories in the Petershams' work that help to keep very young children engrossed in the picture.

OPPOSITE "What you would *seem* to be—be *really*," from *A Bird in the Hand*. A clever illustration demonstrates even to very young children the meaning of a rather complex concept.

What you would *seem* to be –
be *really*

STORY OF THE
PRESIDENTS
of the United States of America

REVISED EDITION

BY MAUD AND MISKA PETERSHAM

The Macmillan Company, New York   Collier-Macmillan Limited, London

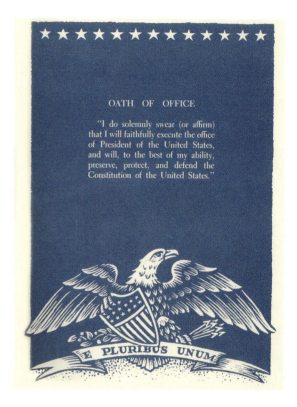

OATH OF OFFICE

"I do solemnly swear (or affirm) that I will faithfully execute the office of President of the United States, and will, to the best of my ability, preserve, protect, and defend the Constitution of the United States."

E PLURIBUS UNUM

Title page for *Story of the Presidents*, a reference book for children of elementary-school age that provides information on each president in chronological order. A starred review in *Library Journal* ensured that this volume would have a place on library shelves for years to come.

The half-title page from *Story of the Presidents*, including the oath of office, the emblematic eagle and the "from many, one" motto.

George Washington
FATHER OF HIS COUNTRY
February 22, 1732   December 14, 1799

FEDERALIST   FIRST PRESIDENT 1789–1797

With the booming of cannons and the ringing of bells, a great shout went up from a throng of people crowding the narrow street or clinging on nearby roof-tops. "LONG LIVE GEORGE WASHINGTON, PRESIDENT OF THE UNITED STATES."

This was in the year 1789. The crowds were gathered in front of Federal Hall in the City of New York. On the balcony of the Hall, above the cheering crowds, stood a tall, dignified man. He was dressed in a dark brown suit with knee breeches and white stockings with silver buckled shoes. His white powdered hair was tied back in a small bag, the fashion of the times. His kindly face was serious as he bowed and acknowledged the cheers of the people.

George Washington had just taken the oath of office as the first President of the United States of America.

7

A typical spread from *Story of the Presidents*—in this case, George Washington. Each president gets two to three pages, with a large illustration, common sobriquet, dates in office, dates of birth and death, political party, and a narrative on his life with a focus on one or two particular incidents.

An illustration from *The Silver Mace*, a fictional history of Williamsburg, Virginia.
This title was published when the ambitious restoration of Colonial Williamsburg,
funded in large part by the Rockefeller family, was substantially completed and
the town was attracting visitors. Maud and Miska spent many weeks there, making
sketches and doing research for *The Silver Mace*.

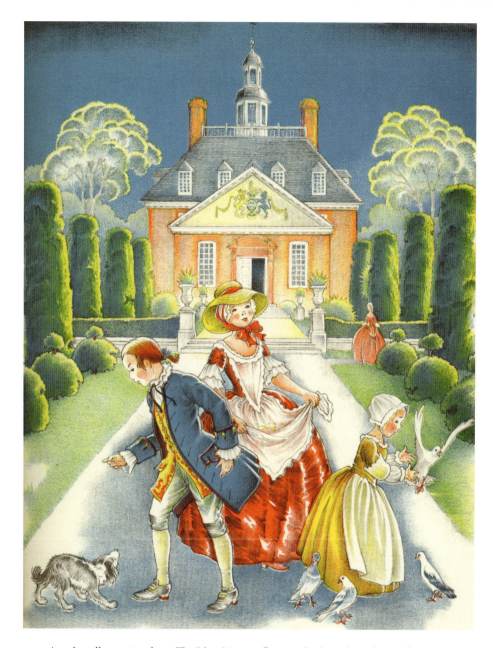

Another illustration from *The Silver Mace*, reflecting the Petershams' careful research on period costumes and settings.

In the open field near the Capitol Miska set up his easel for many days as he painted with infinite patience the rich colors and intricate architectural design of that beautiful building, while Maud found a quiet corner in the Bruton Parish churchyard . . . to make her sketches.
— From *The Title Page*, Macmillan newsletter, 1956

CHAPTER 7

A Grandparent's Perspective

Later Picture Books

This book is for younger children than we usually write for, but when our new grandchild came to our house, we just had to have a book for her. So The Box With Red Wheels *is for our own little grandchild, Mary.*

— Miska Petersham, in an interview
on the *Carnival of Books* radio program, 1952[1]

In the last decade of their extraordinary partnership the Petershams wrote and illustrated six books. These began as stories for very young children, inspired by the birth of their first grandchild, Mary, in 1946 and their second, Mary's brother Michael, in 1950. Mary and Michael were in the vanguard of the baby boomers, a generation that would redefine American culture and one that represented a new view of children and childhood. The years immediately following World War II brought seminal events in American culture: the first edition of Dr. Spock's landmark *The Common Sense Book of Baby and Child Care* (1946), the first *Howdy Doody Show* on NBC (1947), and the patriotism and anti-Communism associated with the Cold War.

My Very First Book: The Story of My First Five Years is a baby book, with spaces for parents to fill in the details by hand and to paste in photographs highlighting their child's first half decade. The prototype for this book was produced for Mary when she was born; Mary's hand-made copy begins with a sketch of the full-color illustration that opens the published book, four angels carrying a sleeping baby in a cradle through a starry sky—the baby on its way to being born.

The book is very much a product of its time. Hospital and birthing practices of the 1940s are suggested by the line "When my mother first saw me I looked like this," illustrated by a very clean and swaddled baby and indicating that the mother had been under some kind of anesthesia during the birth. In addition to time and date of birth and the baby's weight, there are blanks for "the names of my Doctors" and "the Nurses who cared for me." It's a safe world—"People gathered round my crib . . . old and young faces, happy faces, and worried faces stared down at me but they all seemed glad to see me. . . . Everyone has a family tree and this is mine."

A later chapter is "The Outside World," a big and exciting place—the illustration includes

Miska and Maud, circa 1955.

everything from a milk cow and her calf, to a city skyscraper, to an airplane flying over mountains, to a stream with ducks! Sitting right in the middle of this bright world is a slightly older baby—perhaps four or five months—looking full of wonder. Then come "My First Christmas Day," "My First Birthday" and, in more rapid succession, second and third Christmases and birthdays, with a pause for "On my third Christmas they told me a beautiful story about the Baby Jesus in the manger and about a bright shining star." The fourth year includes a page each for favorite toys, favorite books, and pets. Then, in the fifth year, life really starts to happen, with name of school, name of teacher and "names of my very best friends": "Now that I am five I am starting on an exciting adventure. The whole wide world is before me." The accompanying illustration (jacket cover of this book) depicts a girl and boy ascending a long flight of stairs toward a huge door opening onto what looks like a gleaming, magical world—a complement to the opening picture of the baby being carried by angels. The final illustration, on the very last left-hand page, is of a child with a stick and hobo's bundle over his shoulder, walking toward a distant star, alone, and the hand-lettered message "Good Luck." The implication that children leave home at five is quite wonderful, and probably quite unintentional.

The Box With Red Wheels (Macmillan, 1949) is meant for the very young child, perhaps a three- or four-year-old, who has a new sibling. The main character is a silent, sleeping baby who attracts the curiosity of all the farm animals. Reviewers greeted this book happily, but none commented on the fact that it is aimed at a much younger audience than the Petershams' previous work: "These two well known author illustrators have made a charming picture book out of interests consistently appealing to very small children."[2] "The Petershams have produced another completely beautiful picture book for the youngest child."[3]

Miska did state, in an interview on the radio program *Carnival of Books*, that the book was intended for young children. And he suggested as much in a Valentine's Day greeting to his tiny granddaughter, which she has kept to this day; it is a hand-drawn color picture of the dog from the book and a handwritten note: "Watch little doggie, because one of these days he will run in the gate with your

book in his mouth and lots and lots of love from Maudy and Miska."[4]

A year later came *The Circus Baby*, which combines laugh-out-loud humor with an underlying message about being true to oneself. The *New York Times* allotted ample space to this Petersham offering under the heading "Etiquette for Elephants." And its reviewer was impressed: "Although really a sensible sort of pachyderm, Mother Elephant does have one ambition that even her best-of-all babies can't quite satisfy. . . . Maud and Miska Petersham have combined talents again to make a delightful picture book. The four-color circus scenes are bright and simple. Mother and Baby are wonderfully expressive but still quite real elephants, rather than the stuffed toy variety so familiar in the nursery books."[5] That expressiveness combined with realism was hard won. "Sometimes we use other pictures or models," explained Miska. "But in the case of the elephants, it was more of thinking up the motions—how would they do it? Tiptoeing was very difficult. At night I used to wake up and think about how the wrinkles or muscles would move on the elephants tiptoeing."[6]

Maud and Miska saw a lot of their grandchildren. Although Mish and Marj lived away from Woodstock, the family spent extended summers there at the Petershams' home, and the children were very much a part of the daily goings on. In 1954, when *Off to Bed: 7 Stories for Wide-Awakes* was published, Mary was seven and Michael four. This book might have been put together just for little Michael.

Reviewers were mild but approving:

Weary parents who find the bedtime story hour the longest part of the day will welcome these seven brief tales of the animal world. Each story requires only five minutes for reading aloud and contains the simple but important moral that "it's best to follow mother's advice." The little chick who didn't come when his mother called and had to spend a miserable night in the rain wished he had listened. So did the greedy duckling who insisted on having just one more grasshopper and got a bumble bee instead.[7]

Reading this aloud to a child at bedtime, even today, suggests that the Petershams had a finely tuned ear for what is appealing and effective for young children. Perhaps they took pleasure in putting Mary and Michael to bed when they were visiting. These tales have just enough activity to hold a child's interest, just enough information to provide food for thought, and they all end with a feeling of safe harbor and sleepiness.

The Boy Who Had No Heart (1955) is for older children, with illustrations that set the tale squarely in Woodstock, New York, Maud and Miska's hometown. "A new book by this distinguished author-illustrator team is always welcome," commented the *New York Times* critic. "The theme of this one seems somewhat mature for the recommended age level, but 14 good full-page pictures help carry the direct teaching message to younger and older children."[8] The reviewer brings up an interesting point—this book asks a big question: What does it really mean to "have a heart"? It is characteristic of Maud and Miska to not necessarily think this a question over the heads of youngsters.

The Peppernuts (1958) is a chapter book about a large, unorthodox and most inventive family who go off to live in a cabin in the woods, cheerfully unconcerned about how the world might regard their actions. *Kirkus* reviewers liked it very much, one describing it as "a delightful invention of those whimsical Petershams, a happy, vaguely Bohemian family . . . Safe, cozy, and just a little bit zany. Fantasy, balanced by enthusiastic sanity, underlie this domestic circus. Not too much of a story, but such a nice family!"[9] Many of the family's experiences are not unlike those of the Petershams themselves over the course of their lives and travels. The Petershams spent several summers in Canada, on an island in the St. Lawrence River where conditions were almost as they describe for the Peppernut family; they washed their dishes in the river and fashioned their own makeshift furniture.

While these last books—those from 1948 to 1958—are less vivid, less arresting in general, than their earlier works, the Petershams stay true to their themes, balancing adventure with safety, individual with family and community responsibility, and parental care with early independence for children. Even the baby in *The Box With Red Wheels* is left alone in the garden in her cradle; the last page of *My Very First Book* is all about adventure and the future, unencumbered by visible parents, similar to *Miki and Mary*. In *Circus Baby* the message, embodied in the words "after all you are an elephant," is, clearly, to be true to oneself and one's particular gifts. In *The Peppernuts* one of the children, Captain, is depicted as all by himself while in the throes of making a big decision—whether or not to sell his butterfly collection to benefit the dwindling family coffers. Characteristically in the Petershams' work, important moments come when a person is alone—even a very young person.

Important Books in This Chapter

My Very First Book. Macmillan, 1948
The Box With Red Wheels. Macmillan, 1949
The Circus Baby. Macmillan, 1950
Off to Bed: 7 Stories for Wide-Awakes. Macmillan, 1954
The Boy Who Had No Heart. Macmillan, 1955
The Peppernuts. Macmillan, 1958

The first illustration that appears in *My Very First Book: The Story of My First Five Years*. This one depicts the scene just before the baby is born—a nice way to be delivered!

The Beginning
    Once upon a time, to be exact it was at _____ on _____ and in _____,
I was born. — Opening lines of *My Very First Book*

This baby in *My Very First Book* looks not a bit frightened, despite the strange and crowded, bustling world.

The Outside World
   The first time I really saw the outside world was on _____ at _____.
   It was a strange world of many sounds and crowded with all kinds of queer-looking big and little things. — From *My Very First Book*

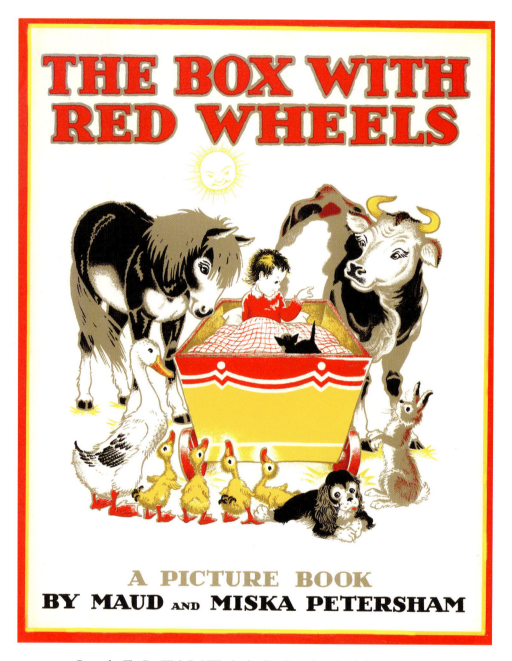

Cover for *The Box With Red Wheels*, the first Petersham book for very young children, inspired by the birth of their first grandchild. The baby has just awakened, to encounter a world of curious and benevolent-looking animals.

The Petershams have produced another completely beautiful picture book for the youngest child. — *Chicago Tribune*

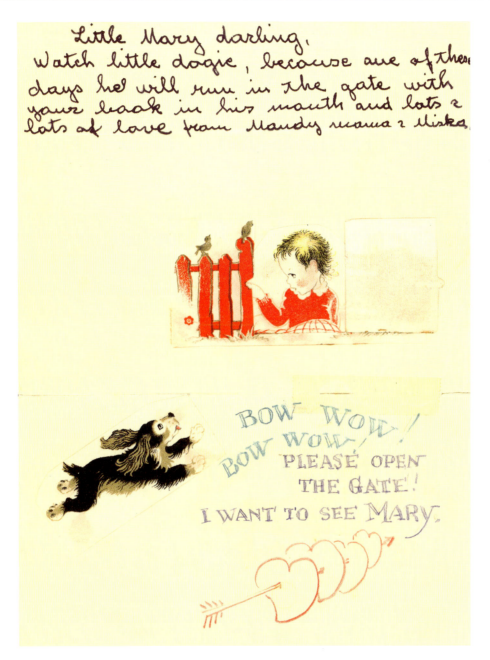

What fun to get a handmade card from your grandfather!
This was made by Miska for his granddaughter, Mary. The flap
to the right of the baby's head opens and closes as the gate.

Illustration from *The Circus Baby*, a rollicking story about a mother elephant whose ambitions for her baby are extreme. She has hopes that he will learn to comport himself in the same way as her friends the clowns. Like so many of the Petershams' illustrations, this one tells small stories that are not in the text. The tiger kitten in the lower right corner often elicits questions from young listeners.

A detailed dummy page from *The Circus Baby* (see illustration at left), once again showing how carefully the Petershams planned their books, sketching details very early in the process. No tiger kitten yet.

OPPOSITE Baby elephant on tiptoe, from *The Circus Baby*. Miska recounted that he lost sleep trying to imagine just how an elephant's muscles and skin would look if the animal stood on tiptoe.

The little elephant took hold of his mother's tail.
Stepping softly, they made their way
across the circus grounds.
They tiptoed right up to the clowns' empty tent.

OFF TO BED

7 STORIES FOR
WIDE-AWAKES

BY
MAUD AND MISKA PETERSHAM

THE MACMILLAN COMPANY
NEW YORK

Title page for *Off to Bed*, a collection of seven very short tales about how various animals end their day. At this time, Maud and Miska's two young grandchildren spent long weeks at their house, and the book reflects very real experience in helping youngsters make the transition from active daytime to sleepy nighttime.

OPPOSITE "The Bear Cubs," from *Off to Bed*. Although the bears are drawn in a way that is appealing to children, the Petershams' careful research is apparent in the anatomical details of the animals. Also on this page is an illuminated initial capital, a Petersham hallmark throughout their career.

THE BEAR CUBS

Susie and Johnny Bear lived in a snug warm hole in a hollow tree. They were more than two months old but they had never yet been out of the hole.

Mother Bear spent most of her time sleeping. The little cubs spent most of their time sleeping too, cuddled up close beside her.

It was always dark in the little den.

Illustration from *The Boy Who Had No Heart*, the tale of a little boy who is so disagreeable that his parents take him to the family doctor—who diagnoses lack of heart as the problem. Throughout the story, the boy looks all over for a heart, and in this illustration is rejoicing in finally finding it through lessons learned. People who know Woodstock, New York, the Petershams' hometown, will recognize this as the village green. The mountain in the background is called Overlook, and it is believed by some people in this artists' colony to be imbued with magic powers.

This woodland setting from *The Peppernuts* appears in *Auntie*, as well as in other books by the Petershams.

Here, Captain, one of four Peppernut children, in solitary retreat from his busy family, struggles to reach an important decision.

The Legacy of Maud and Miska Petersham

Like toys, books for children reflect surely the
temper of the period into which they are born.
— E. B. White [1]

Let your life speak. — Parker Palmer [2]

The Petershams' legacy is tangible, right there on the bookshelf—but it is also intangible, resting in the facts of their lives, in the remarkable partnership they formed early and lived long.

During their lifetimes, their work was praised by critics, honored by librarians, enjoyed by children, sought by publishers. Today, scholars of children's literature recognize the Petershams as important leaders at a significant time in the history of American publishing. They are remembered for their internationalism, their technical innovations, and the artistry and beauty of their illustrations. Their books today are of historical interest to bibliophiles, nostalgic interest to adults of a certain age, and fresh interest to children who are lucky enough to encounter them for the first time.

The Petershams worked through times of great change—the shell-shocked late Tens, the Roaring Twenties, the gloomy and austere Thirties, the freshly patriotic Forties, the Cold War Fifties. Their books throughout these decades tacitly reflect unchanging values, without oversimplifying them. The hope and joy of science and technology are leavened with appreciation for the more mysterious, spiritual realm; wild adventures are made possible by knowledge of safe harbor at home; individualism and self-reliance are tempered with nurturing of family and community; patriotism is enriched by a global sensibility. The books speak for themselves.

So, too, do their lives speak. Maud's Quaker ancestors had a saying: "Let your life preach," often recast today as "Let your life speak." Among the multiple layers of meaning in this simple idea is the notion that one's actions and way of life are as important as anything one says. Maud and Miska's lives did indeed speak—of hard work, of extended family, of community, of research and learning, of patriotism, of love of nature. They lived with a kind of radical integrity, in the sense that the multiple parts of their lives fit together into an integrated whole, informed, always, by a sense of humor and a sense of perspective.

Miska embodies one of America's favorite hero myths—the impoverished immigrant arriving on our shores, quickly carving out an admirably successful life through hard work and skill. Maud embodies another, quite different, American myth—that of a new American aristocracy based on *Mayflower* roots, spiritual rigor, a Protestant work ethic, and prestigious education. Irene Smith wrote simply, "Nothing about this perfect collaboration is more amazing than the fact that it began."[3]

But begin it did, centered first on the wish of each of them to find a life and a living in art. Both spoke of wanting to draw and paint from the time they were children. They both embodied another popular myth—that one of the keys to a good life is to find your passion, to "follow your bliss."[4] Following that bliss brought them together in New York, at a time when the very definitions of "art" were being challenged, and when commercial art in advertising and book illustration was burgeoning. They quickly developed a partnership—in life and in work—so strong that it is difficult to imagine either of them alone producing work of the volume and quality they did together.

They gravitated to the small artists' community of Woodstock, New York, and added to its variety and excitement. Theirs was not an insular "us against the world" kind of partnership. People who knew them remember a warm, open, welcoming household, with good food and good conversation. The house itself reflected their artistic work—in their collected artifacts tucked into nooks and crannies everywhere, in Miska's furniture, in Maud's ceramics.

Maud and Miska's legacy of good work and of lives well lived is important today, when the pace of change is literally mind-blowing; communications technology is changing our very consciousness. Surrounded by unfiltered stimulus and too much data and too many choices, the notion of steering one's life and work by a few fixed stars is not only comforting but useful.

Frontispiece from *Get-A-Way*, a visual summary of the story of two decrepit toys entering a magic land whence they emerge good as new— but only after many tests of their strength, ingenuity and character.

NOTES

"The de Grummond Collection" refers to Maud and Miska Petersham Papers, de Grummond Children's Literature Collection, University of Southern Mississippi Libraries.

For the *New York Times* citations refer to the NYT Article Archive.

Image caption notes follow text notes for each chapter:
Page number + L = left; R = right; T = top; B = bottom.

PROLOGUE Different Journeys, Same Destination

1   Maud Petersham, typescript, circa 1939. The de Grummond Collection, box 1, folder 4.

CHAPTER 1 Artful Lives

1   Maud and Miska Petersham interview with Rex Frost (CFRB, Toronto, 1948). Transcription in de Grummond Collection, box 3, folder 4. Rex Frost was a broadcaster in Toronto from 1927 through the 1940s. For more information about Frost and CFRB, see http://www.broadcasting-history.ca/index3.html.

2   Mary Petersham Reinhard, conversation with the author, August 11, 2011.

3   For a comprehensive history of American Quakerism and its relationship to other Protestant sects, see Howard H. Brinton's *Friends for 350 Years* (Wallingford, Pa.: Pendle Hill, 2002).

4   Information on Maud's forbears is compiled from a variety of sources, including Celia Jane Sisson's unpublished autobiography, written in 1941 (photocopy of typescript provided to the author by Mary Petersham Reinhard), and a scrapbook that Maud prepared for her granddaughter in the 1960s. Collection of Mary Petersham Reinhard.

5   Accessed September 11, 2011, on the Mount Holyoke College Web site: http://www.mtholyoke.edu/marylyon/accomplishments.html.

6   Sisson, op. cit., 40.

7   Alexander King Sisson, "A Youth's Conversation With Himself." An address to the students of Afton Academy, June 25, 1882. Manuscript in de Grummond Collection, box 1, folder 5.

8   Dana R. Bailey, "Reverend Andrew King Fuller Biography." In *History of Minnehaha County, SD* (Sioux Falls, S.D.: Brown & Sanger, 1899). See http://files.usgwarchives.net/sd/minnehaha/history/bailey/bios/fuller.txt.

9   Lee Bennett Hopkins, *Books Are by People: Interviews With 104 Authors and Illustrators of Books for Young Children* (New York: Citation, 1969), 210–15.

10 Mitzi Shewmake, conversation with the author, February 11, 2010.

11 Hopkins, op. cit., 211.

12 Sisson, op. cit., 73–74.

13 Mary Petersham Reinhard, conversation with the author, August 11, 2011.

14 Hopkins, op. cit., 212.

15 Sharyl G. Smith, *Maud and Miska Petersham: Their Work in American Children's Book Publishing, 1920–1939*. Unpublished doctoral dissertation, Columbia University, 1985, 27.

16 *The Overlook*, Woodstock, N.Y., August 1, 1931, 7.

17 Maud, "Stories of Miska." Typescript in de Grummond Collection, box 1, folder 2.

18 Maud, letter to Doris Patee, 1960. Photocopy provided to the author by Mitzi Shewmake.

19 Manuscript in Miska's hand. Speech prepared for National Book Week, 1946: "Books Are Bridges." The de Grummond Collection, box 1, folder 1.

20 Frost interview, op. cit.

21 Undated typescript, with note in Maud's handwriting at the bottom: "That was Miska's First Picture." The de Grummond Collection, box 1, folder 3.

22 Maud to Doris Patee, op. cit.

23 Ibid.

24 Letter from Ernö Balogh to Maud and Miska in

de Grummond Collection, box 4, folder, 4. Miska and Ernö became estranged when Ernö married Malvina Schweizer, an American biology professor with socialist beliefs. Miska was at that time an ardent anti-Communist. Mitzi Shewmake, conversation with the author, December 21, 2011.

25 Maud to Doris Patee, op. cit.

26 Ibid.

27 Ibid.

28 Mary Petersham Reinhard, conversation with the author, August 11, 2011, and Mitzi Shewmake, conversation with the author, December 21, 2011.

29 Notebook in de Grummond Collection, box 4, folder 8.

30 Harold Rosenberg, "The Armory Show: Revolution Reenacted," The Art Galleries, *New Yorker*, April 6, 1963, 99.

31 Christopher Long, *Paul T. Frankl and Modern American Design* (New Haven, Conn.: Yale University Press, 2007), 27–29.

32 *New York Times*, April 2, 1914.

33 Irene Smith Green, typescript, 8. (The article appeared in *Horn Book Magazine*, July 1946.) The de Grummond Collection, box 3, folder 4.

34 Sisson, op. cit., 88.

35 *New York Times*, February 5, 1919.

36 "Certificate of Discharge from Military Service," September 16, 1917. The de Grummond Collection, box 1, folder 6.

37 From Charles E. Gradwell, comp., *Facts and Figures About Our Town* [pamphlet] (Woodstock, N.Y.: The Overlook, 1941).

38 Sisson, op. cit., 90.

39 Ibid.

40 For comprehensive treatments of Byrdcliffe and Woodstock, see Anita M. Smith, *Woodstock History and Hearsay*, 2nd ed. (Woodstock, N.Y.: WoodstockArts, 2006); Alf Evers, *Woodstock: History of an American Town* (Woodstock, N.Y.: Overlook Press, 1987); and Nancy E. Green, ed., *Byrdcliffe: An American Arts and Crafts Colony* (Ithaca, N.Y.: Cornell University Press, 2004).

41 Maud Petersham, "Illustrating Books for Children." *Elementary English Review* 2 (March), 1925: 85–88.

42 Orville H. Peets, "Maud and Miska Petersham: A Note About Their Work." *Woodstock Bulletin*, 1920, 10–11. Benjamin Day was the inventor of the commonly used Ben-Day Dots color printing process.

43 Petersham, "Illustrating Books for Children," op. cit., 85.

44 Peets, op. cit.

45 Aileen Fletcher McFee, "Roster of Woodstock Artists." *Publications of the Woodstock Historical Society*, 1930, 22–23.

46 "My Food Book." Bound journal of Maud's. Collection of Mary Petersham Reinhard.

47 Maud to Wilna Hervey and Nan Mason, February 1930s. Wilna Hervey and Nan Mason papers, Smithsonian Archives of American Art. Online summary of the collection: www.aaa.si.edu/collections/wilna-hervey-and-nan-mason-papers-15628.

48 Evers, op. cit., 650. Peter Whitehead, Jane's son, actually inherited Byrdcliffe; on his death in 1976, he left it to the Woodstock Guild of Craftsmen, Inc., and named a committee of similar makeup but different people, since many of those on his mother's list had passed on.

49 Frances Rogers, *The Story of a Small Town Library: The Development of the Woodstock, N.Y. Library* (Woodstock, N.Y.: Overlook Press, 1974).

50 It should be noted that in fact there have been several creative husband-and-wife teams in children's book publishing, some contemporary with Maud and Miska. For example, two couples, Berta and Elmer Hader and Alice and Martin Provensen, were contemporary with the Petershams, and today there are the recent Caldecott winners Erin Stead and Philip Stead.

51 Handwritten note by Maud. The de Grummond Collection, box 1, folder 1.

52 Maud, typescript (hand-lettered at top, "For Lee Bennett Hopkins Books are By People"), n.d. The de Grummond Collection, box 1, folder 1.

53 Handwritten note by Maud. The de Grummond Collection, box 1, folder 1.

54 Mitzi Shewmake, conversation with the author, February 11, 2010.

55 Mitzi Shewmake, conversation with the author, December 21, 2011.

56 Frost interview, op. cit. "Mr. Petersham is literally your right-hand man," said Frost, the interviewer.

57 Handwritten note. The de Grummond Collection, box 3, folder 2.

58   Selma G. Lanes, *Down the Rabbit Hole: Adventures and Misadventures in the Realm of Children's Literature* (New York: Atheneum, 1971), 59.

59   Maud, typescript, no annotation. The de Grummond Collection, box 1, folder 1.

60   Handwritten letter from Miska to Maud, n.d. Collection of Mary Petersham Reinhard.

61   Sharyl G. Smith, op. cit., 55.

62   Maud to Wilna Hervey and Nan Mason, March 3, 1959. Smithsonian Archives of American Art, op. cit.

63   Mary Petersham Reinhard, conversation with the author, August 11, 2011.

64   Mitzi Shewmake, conversation with the author, February 11, 2010.

65   Maud, typescript, n.d. (1930s). The de Grummond Collection, box 3, folder 1.

66   Handwritten note from Miska to Maud, n.d. Collection of Mary Petersham Reinhard.

67   Quoted in Walt Reed, comp., *The Illustrator in America, 1900–1960s* (New York: Reinhold, 1966), 267.

68   Reed, op. cit., 6.

69   Maud to Doris Patee, op. cit.

70   *New York Times* accounts of American Institute of Graphic Arts shows, December 5, 1926, and November 28, 1933.

71   Frost interview, op. cit.

72   Handwritten note from Bechtel to Maud and Miska, 1946. The de Grummond Collection, box 3, folder 4.

73   Grumbacher ad, *Art Digest*, October 1948. Proof in de Grummond Collection, box 3, folder 5.

74   Maud to Wilna Hervey and Nan Mason from 32 Bank Street, New York City, March 3, 1945. Smithsonian Archives of American Art, op. cit.

75   Handwritten note from Miska to Mary Petersham. Collection of Mary Petersham Reinhard.

76   Handwritten letter and notes on Miska's life from Maud to Doris Patee, written from Miska's hospital room in Alexandria, Virginia, in 1960, shortly before his death.

77   Handwritten note by Maud. Collection of Mary Petersham Reinhard.

78   Patee to Maud, May 16, 1960. The de Grummond Collection, box 2, folder 5.

79   Sharyl G. Smith, op. cit.

80   Hopkins, op. cit., 211.

81   Typescript headed "1946—Maud Petersham." The de Grummond Collection, box 3, folder 3.

Caption Notes

FRONTISPIECE   Enclosure in a letter from Maud to Doris Patee just prior to Miska's death. Collection of Mitzi Shewmake.

7   Letter from John Striebel to Maud and Miska, n.d. The de Grummond Collection, box 2, folder 1.

15   Lee Bennett Hopkins, *Books Are by People: Interviews With 104 Authors and Illustrators of Books for Young Children* (New York: Citation, 1969), 210.

17   Ibid., 211.

18   Scrapbook prepared by Maud for her granddaughter, Mary Petersham Reinhard, in the 1960s.

20T   Handwritten note. The de Grummond Collection, box 1, folder 2.

20B   Maud, in a handwritten note. The de Grummond Collection, box 1, folder 2.

21T   Handwritten note, n.d. The de Grummond Collection, box 1, folder 2.

25   Ibid.

33   Maud, bound journal, "My Food Book," 1938–1958. Collection of Mary Petersham Reinhard.

CHAPTER 2   **Hardworking Artists**

1   Quoted by Ellean Eayres of Harcourt, Brace in a letter to Maud, November 1, 1922. The de Grummond Collection, box 4, folder 3.

2   Quoted in Lee Bennett Hopkins, *Books Are by People: Interviews With 104 Authors and Illustrators of Books for Young Children* (New York: Citation, 1969), 211.

3   Pogány's career included not only illustrations for books, magazines and advertising, but also public murals, set design for the Metropolitan Opera and books about illustration technique. He was four years Miska's senior and had had a successful start in London and New York by the time Miska arrived in New York in 1912.

4   Typescript of "American Library Association Newbery and Caldecott Award Presentations From Statler Hotel, Buffalo, NY, June 18, 1946"—introductory remarks by Frederic G. Melcher. The de Grummond Collection, box 3, folder 3. Melcher (1879–1963), long-time editor of *Publishers' Weekly* and a great champion of children's books, was instrumental in establishing both awards. He was one of the most important bookmen of his generation.

5   Celia Jane Sisson autobiography. Unpublished

manuscript, 1941, 89. Photocopy provided to the author by Mary Petersham Reinhard.

6 Edward Robinson to Miska, February 2, 1926. The de Grummond Collection, box 4, folder 2.

7 Leonard S. Marcus, *Minders of Make-Believe: Idealists, Entrepreneurs, and the Shaping of American Children's Literature* (New York: Houghton Mifflin, 2008), 91.

8 Maud, draft for tribute to May Massee. The de Grummond Collection, box 3, folder 2.

9 Miska to Mitzi and Ed Shewmake, 1950. Quoted in Sharyl G. Smith, "Maud and Miska Petersham: Their Work in American Children's Book Publishing, 1920–1939." Unpublished doctoral thesis, Columbia University, 1985, 69.

10 Marcus, op. cit., 96.

11 Ibid., 77.

12 Letter from Louise Seaman Bechtel to Maud and Miska. The de Grummond Collection, box 3, folder 3.

13 Letter from Bertha E. Mahony to Maud, September 30, 1919. The de Grummond Collection, box 4, folder 2.

14 Letter from Frances Ross to Maud and Miska, July 21, 1923. The de Grummond Collection, box 4, folder 3.

15 Letter from Mabel G. La Rue to Maud and Miska, March 3, 1927. The de Grummond Collection, box 4, folder 1.

16 Letter from James Snowden to Maud and Miska, September 23, 1919. The de Grummond Collection, box 4, folder 1.

17 Letter from Mary L. B. Branch to Bertha Mahony, publisher of *Guld: The Cavern King,* December 10, 1919. The de Grummond Collection, box 4, folder 1.

18 Letter from Miriam E. Mason to Maud and Miska, November 10, 1941. The de Grummond Collection, box 2, folder 7.

19 Maud Petersham, "Illustrating Books for Children." *Elementary English Review* 2 (March), 1925, 87.

20 Maud, typescript (hand-lettered at top, "For Lee Bennett Hopkins Books are By People"), n.d. The de Grummond Collection, box 1, folder 1.

21 Barbara Bader, *American Picturebooks From Noah's Ark to the Beast Within* (New York: Macmillan,

1976), 38. Bader refers to Bertha Mahony Miller and Elinor Whitney Field, eds., *Realms of Gold in Children's Books* (Garden City, N.Y.: Doubleday, 1929).

Caption Notes

53 The de Grummond Collection, box 4, folder 8.

55 Leonard S. Marcus, *Minders of Make-Believe: Idealists, Entrepreneurs, and the Shaping of American Children's Literature* (New York: Houghton Mifflin, 2008), 91.

59 Letter from E. K. Robinson, Ginn & Co. to Miska, December 19, 1926. The de Grummond Collection, box 1, folder 5.

60 Maud Petersham, "Illustrating Books for Children," *Elementary English Review*, August 1926, 87.

61 Letter to Maud and Miska from Mary L. B. Branch, 1918. The de Grummond Collection, box 4, folder 2.

63 Barbara Bader, *American Picturebooks From Noah's Ark to the Beast Within* (New York: Macmillan, 1976), 38. Letter from Frances Marshall: de Grummond Collection, box 4, folder 2.

64-65 Carl Sandburg, *Rootabaga* Stories (New York: Harcourt, Brace, 1922), frontispiece; letter from D. C. Brace to Maud; letter from Carl Sandburg to D. C. Brace. The de Grummond Collection, box 4, folders 1 and 3.

65L Letter from Carl Sandburg to D. C. Brace. The de Grummond Collection, box 4, folder 1.

65R Letter from Carl Sandburg to D. C. Brace. The de Grummond Collection, box 4, folder 3.

68 Anita Silvey, ed., *Children's Books and Their Creators: An Invitation to the Feast of Twentieth-Century Children's Literature* (New York: Houghton Mifflin Harcourt, 1995), 531.

74 *Maria, Queen Consort of Ferdinand, King of Romania* (New York: Frederick A. Stokes, 1929).

75 Maud, handwritten note. The de Grummond Collection, box 1, folder 2.

77R Letter from Miriam E. Mason to Maud. The de Grummond Collection, box 2, folder 2.

CHAPTER 3 **All Ours**

1 Lee Bennett Hopkins, *Books Are by People: Interviews With 104 Authors and Illustrators of Books for Young Children* (New York: Citation, 1969), 210.

2   Handwritten letter to Petershams on Doubleday stationery. Undated but probably 1929, the year of publication of *Miki*. The de Grummond Collection, box 1, folder 1.

3   Maud Petersham, *Chicago Sun*, November 19, 1946. The de Grummond Collection, box 4, folder 1.

4   Hopkins, op. cit., 211.

5   Massee to Maud and Miska, February 24, 1928. The de Grummond Collection, box 4, folder 2.

6   Maud Petersham, "May Massee as Her Author-Illustrators See Her." *Horn Book Magazine*, July-August 1936, 230ff.

7   Anita Silvey, *Children's Books and Their Creators* (New York: Houghton Mifflin, 1995), 518.

8   Hopkins, op. cit., 211.

9   Miller to Petershams, December 5, 1932. The de Grummond Collection, box 4, folder 1.

10 May Lamberton Becker, "Books for Young People." *New York Herald Tribune*, October 22, 1933. The de Grummond Collection, box 4, folder 1.

11 As did several of her important authors, among them Robert McCloskey, Kurt Wiese, and Ingri and Edgar Parin D'Aulaire.

12 Handwritten note from Massee to Maud and Miska on Viking notepaper, n.d. but probably 1931 or 1932. The de Grummond Collection, box 4, folder 2.

13 Personal communication from Mary Prevo and Simrat Kaur Khalsa to the author, April 2011.

14 Cornelia Meigs, ed., *A Critical History of Children's Literature*, rev. ed. (New York: Macmillan, 1969), 649.

15 Leonard S. Marcus, *Minders of Make-Believe: Idealists, Entrepreneurs, and the Shaping of American Children's Literature* (New York: Houghton Mifflin, 2008), 95.

16 Irene Smith Green, manuscript for "Maud and Miska Petersham." The de Grummond Collection, box 3, folder 4, and *Horn Book Magazine*, July 1946.

17 Personal communication from Mary Petersham Reinhard and Mitzi Shewmake to the author, and author memory.

18 Handwritten note dated August 15, 1935, Stockbridge, Massachusetts. The de Grummond Collection, box 4, folder 4.

19 Oscar Dannenberg, *Bridgeport Life*, November 24, 1934. The de Grummond Collection, box 4, folder 1.

Caption Notes

84-85 May Massee to Maud. The de Grummond Collection, box 3, folder 2.

85B Maud Petersham, "May Massee as Her Author-Illustrators See Her" (*Horn Book Magazine*, July–August 1936), 230.

87   Letter from May Massee to Maud and Miska, February 24, 1928. The de Grummond Collection, box 4, folder 2.

88-89 Maud, from a typescript, 1939. The de Grummond Collection, box 1, folder 2.

98   Maud Petersham, "Traveling in Picture Book Places" (*Young Wings: The Magazine of the Boys' Own Club*, Junior Guild, November 1934), 10.

100 *Davenport Daily Times*, November 10, 1934. The de Grummond Collection, box 3, folder 6.

CHAPTER 4 **Illuminating the Bible**

1   Maud, typescript for a speech. The de Grummond Collection, box 1, folder 3.

2   Personal communication to the author from Mary Prevo, Simrat Khalsa, Gioja Brislawn and others, April 2011.

3   Cornelia Meigs, ed., *A Critical History of Children's Literature*, rev. ed. (New York: Macmillan, 1969), 441.

4   *New York Times*, December 13, 1931.

5   Maud Petersham, "Traveling in Picture Book Places." *Young Wings*, 1934, 10–11.

6   Personal communication from Mitzi Shewmake and Mary Petersham Reinhard to the author and author memory.

7   For more about Petersham books published by John C. Winston in this manner, see *The Story Book of . . .* series in chapter 5.

8   Eugenia M. Frost to Maud and Miska, December 8, 1931. The de Grummond Collection, box 4, folder 3.

9   *Ulster County* (New York) *News*, November 17, 1938.

10 Handwritten note by Maud, n.d. The de Grummond Collection, box 33, folder 4.

11 In this treatment, they based the text on the Confraternity of Christian Doctrine edition. The

CCD is a religious-education arm of the Catholic Church, but this book was published as a trade title by Macmillan and was not endorsed by or distributed through any particular denomination.

12 Personal communication from Mary Petersham Reinhard to the author, August 13, 2011.

13 Howard H. Brinton, *Friends for 300 Years: The History and Beliefs of the Society of Friends Since George Fox Started the Quaker Movement* (New York: Harper, 1952).

14 Handwritten letter from Janet Layavoniovich to Maud and Miska, dated March 23, 1946, Readville, Massachusetts. The de Grummond Collection, box 2, folder 8.

Caption Notes

108 Letter from Della MacGregor to the Petershams, circa 1930. The de Grummond Collection, box 4, folder 4.

112L Maud and Miska Petersham interview with Rex Frost (CFRB, Toronto, 1948). Transcription in de Grummond Collection, box 3, folder 4. Rex Frost was a broadcaster in Toronto from 1927 through the 1940s. For more information about Frost and CFRB, go to http://www.broadcasting-history.ca/index3.html.

112R Letter from Maud Cadman to the Petershams, December 4, 1935. The de Grummond Collection, box 4, folder 4.

113 Handwritten note, n.d. The de Grummond Collection, box 1, folder 1.

114 Helen H. Shotwell, "Recapture Feeling of Old Illuminated Manuscripts" (*Ulster County* [New York] *News*, November 17, 1938), 13.

115L Handwritten note from Maud, n.d. The de Grummond Collection, box 1, folder 1.

116L Maud Petersham, "A Dream Comes True" (*Young Wings: The Magazine of the Boys' Own Club*, Junior Guild, July 1938), 10.

116R Ibid., 11.

117 *New York Herald Tribune*, October 16, 1938. The de Grummond Collection box 3, folder 7.

119L Handwritten note from Maud, circa 1940. The de Grummond Collection, box 1, folder 1.

119R Helen H. Shotwell, 1938. The de Grummond Collection, box 3, folder 7.

120 *New York Herald Tribune*, November 15, 1942. The de Grummond Collection, box 3, folder 7.

122 *Marin Independent Journal*, May 18, 1963. The de Grummond Collection, box 3, folder 9.

123 *Winston-Salem Journal*, February 24, 1963. The de Grummond Collection, box 3, folder 9.

CHAPTER 5 **The World Around Us**

1 Sarah L. Rueter, in Barbara Bader, *American Picturebooks From Noah's Ark to the Beast Within* (New York: Macmillan, 1976), 94.

2 Ibid.

3 Cornelia Meigs, ed., *A Critical History of Children's Literature*, rev. ed. (New York: Macmillan, 1969), 621.

4 Miska, *Carnival of Books* radio show, 1952. MP3 file provided to the author by Mitzi Shewmake.

5 Rueter, op. cit., 93.

6 Ibid.

7 Letter from Betty Schiltz to Maud and Miska. The de Grummond Collection, box 2, folder 3.

8 Miska, *Carnival of Books* radio show, 1952, op. cit.

9 Flier from Winifred Fuller Byrd. Collection of Mitzi Shewmake.

10 Letter from Julius R. Ross, President, Southern Rice Sales Company, to the Petershams, December 22, 1936. The de Grummond Collection, box 4, folder 4.

11 Memo to Mr. Kent from J. W. Ziegler on John C. Winston letterhead, December 18, 1934, with Maud's handwritten notes attached. The de Grummond Collection, box 2, folder 2.

12 *New York Times*, February 25, 1940.

13 Rueter, op. cit., 95.

Caption Notes

125 Silvey, op. cit., 533.

129 Bader, op. cit., 94.

130L Ibid., 93.

136 Letter from Arthur L. Erlanger to the Petershams. The de Grummond Collection, box 2, folder 3.

CHAPTER 6 **Appreciating America**

1 Miska, Caldecott acceptance speech, 1946. The de Grummond Collection, box 3, folder 3.

2 Leonard S. Marcus and Children's Book Council, *75 Years of Children's Book Week Posters: Celebrating Great Illustrators of American Children's Books* (New York: Knopf, 1994), 24.

3   Irene Smith Green, typescript, p. 10 (the article appeared in *Horn Book Magazine*, July 1946). The de Grummond Collection, box 3, folder 4.

4   May Lamberton Becker, *New York Herald Tribune*, November 2, 1941. The de Grummond Collection, box 4, folder 2.

5   Letter from "The Boys and Girls of the Pingree School" to Maud and Miska, October 31, 1941. The de Grummond Collection, box 2, folder 7.

6   Maud, Caldecott acceptance speech, 1946. The de Grummond Collection, box 3, folder 1. Published in *Horn Book Magazine*, July 1946, 323ff.

7   Miska, Caldecott acceptance speech, op. cit.

8   Maud, Caldecott acceptance speech, op. cit.

9   Nancy Larrick, "The All-White World of Children's Books." *Saturday Review*, September 11, 1965, 63–65, 84–85.

10 Leonard S. Marcus, *Minders of Make-Believe: Idealists, Entrepreneurs, and the Shaping of American Children's Literature* (New York: Houghton Mifflin, 2008), 233–36.

11 Susan Carr Hirschman to Maud, January 14, 1966. The de Grummond Collection, box 2, folder 2.

12 Myra Cohn Livingston, *Twentieth Century Children's Writers* (New York: St. Martin's Press, 1978), 992.

13 Maud, typescript, with the title "About Making America's Stamps" in Maud's handwriting. Unpaginated. The de Grummond Collection, box 1, folder 2.

14 Maud, typescript, circa 1946. The de Grummond Collection, box 1, folder 2.

15 *Philadelphia Inquirer*, March 23, 1947. The de Grummond Collection, box 3, folder 6.

16 *New York Herald Tribune*, March 23, 1947. The de Grummond Collection, box 3, folder 6.

17 *New York Times*, January 13, 1952.

18 *Library Journal*, May 1, 1953. The de Grummond Collection, box 3, folder 9.

19 *Newport News Daily Press*, June 3, 1956. The de Grummond Collection, box 3, folder 9.

20 The de Grummond Collection, box 4, folder 8.

Caption Notes

139 Irene Smith Green, typescript for article in *Horn Book Magazine*, April 1946. The de Grummond Collection, box 3, folder 4.

146 Miska, Caldecott acceptance speech (*Horn Book Magazine*, July 1946), 245.

149R Ibid., 246.

150 Maud, typescript with the title "About Making America's Stamps," in Maud's handwriting. Unpaginated. The de Grummond Collection, box 1, folder 2.

157 *The Title Page* (Macmillan newsletter), 1956. The de Grummond Collection, box 3, file 9.

CHAPTER 7 A Grandparent's Perspective

1   Miska Petersham, in an interview on the *Carnival of Books* radio program, 1952. MP3 file provided to the author by Mitzi Shewmake.

2   *New York Times*, October 23, 1949.

3   *Chicago Tribune*, November 13, 1949. The de Grummond Collection, box 3, folder 6.

4   Greeting card handmade by Miska for his granddaughter, Mary.

5   *New York Times Book Review*, October 1, 1950. *New York Times* online archives: www.nytimes.com.

6   Miska, in an interview on the *Carnival of Books* radio program, 1952. MP3 file provided to the author by Mitzi Shewmake.

7   *New York Times*, November 14, 1954.

8   *New York Times*, August 7, 1955.

9   *Kirkus Reviews*, August 1958. The de Grummond Collection, box 3, folder 6.

Caption Notes

164 *Chicago Tribune*, November 13, 1949. The de Grummond Collection, box 3, folder 6.

EPILOGUE The Legacy of Maud and Miska Petersham

1   Quoted in Selma G. Lanes, *Down the Rabbit Hole: Adventures and Misadventures in the Realm of Children's Literature* (New York: Atheneum, 1971), 21.

2   Parker Palmer, *Let Your Life Speak: Listening for the Voice of Vocation* (San Francisco: Jossey-Bass, 2000).

3   Irene Smith Green, "Maud and Miska Petersham." *Horn Book Magazine*, July 1946.

4   Joseph Campbell, a popular twentieth-century mythologist, known best for *The Power of Myth*, a PBS television series hosted by Bill Moyers.

LIST OF ILLUSTRATIONS

Page number + L = left; R = right; T = top; B = bottom.

Endpapers from Maud's first illustration commission, for *The Cambridge Book of Poetry for Children*.

ACKNOWLEDGMENTS

SOURCES

The riches available through the Internet have eased the conduct of research. But much of the work on this book relied on very old-fashioned material—unpublished and uncataloged manuscripts, interviews with family, and carefully preserved archival and family records. I am especially indebted to the following:

• Mary Petersham Reinhard, who provided me with amazing riches—not only family photos and original art, but also the typescript of the 1941 autobiography of Celia Jane Sisson, the beloved "Auntie" who had a major hand in raising Maud, and in the household of Maud and Miska from their marriage until Auntie's death.

• Mitzi Shewmake, Maud's niece, who spent much of her childhood with the Petershams and generously shared with me her materials and memories.

• Sharyl Smith, whose 1987 doctoral dissertation is the only comprehensive treatment of the life and work of the Petershams.

• The unparalleled archive of the de Grummond Children's Literature Collection, University of Southern Mississippi Libraries—and particularly Ellen Ruffin, who presides as able and helpful curator.

ENCOURAGEMENT, ENRICHMENT AND SUPPORT

Many long-time friends and colleagues supported me throughout the development of this project with suggestions, reading and encouragement. I am especially grateful to the following:

• Bob Wyatt, who recognized the potential value of the story of the Petershams from the very beginning.

• Candace Butler, who read early daily snippets and responded enthusiastically enough to keep me going.

• Grace Greene and Daniel Greene, for good judgment; their enormous appreciation of children's literature is contagious and everlasting.

• Harriett Barton, who helped me to understand the intricacies of color printing processes and whose expert eye and talent for explaining things helped me to appreciate the work of the Petershams even more.

• My family: Mary Prevo, for her good cheer and archivist's soul; Simrat Kaur Khalsa, for sharing her vivid memories of the Petershams' books and keeping them alive through the next generation; and Barbara Carlson, for all her memories and unconditional cheerleading. My son, Wyatt Roberts, for providing me with many hours of reading pleasure when he was a little boy,

This 1931 poster is the first of three the Petershams produced for Children's Book Week. The internationalist theme here is typical of much of children's publishing—and the Petershams' own work—at the time. Their later posters, done just before and just after World War II, reflect different themes.

and, after he grew up, with gainful employment so I could undertake this project.

• Michael Gotkin, who took the time to cheer me on and help me out.

• Gergely Romsics of the Hungarian Cultural Center in New York, for his quick translation and his early interest.

• Woodstock's venerable cultural institutions and their dedicated staff (past and present), especially JoAnn Margolis at the Historical Society of Woodstock, Emily Jones and Josephine Bloodgood at the Woodstock Artists Association and Museum, and Amy Raff and Pia Alexander at the Woodstock Public Library.

• Samantha Hastings at the University of South Carolina Library School, a great friend and leader, who helped me to put my hands on some very hard-to-capture material.

• Weston Blelock and Julia Blelock, the formidable brother and sister co-publishers at WoodstockArts, whose faith in this project often outmatched mine, and kept me going all the way through with gentle nudges and, sometimes, with loud cracking of whips. (If this book has a single error in sourcing or detail, it is absolutely *not* because of them—their attention to detail is

reminiscent of the dedication of the legendary Harold Ross at *The New Yorker*.)

• Abigail Sturges, art book designer extraordinaire, for her skill, polish and fabulous sense of humor.

• Neal Porter, who took the time to talk with me about this project and helped me to get in touch with Philip and Erin Stead, authors of the Foreword to this volume.

• And—of course—Philip and Erin Stead, representatives of the next generation of husband-and-wife children's book artists, for so graciously looking at the manuscript and providing the Foreword.

The first draft was completed while I was on retreat at Pendle Hill, a Quaker Study Center in Wallingford, Pennsylvania—a remarkable place to focus, get down to work and finish things.

This book is dedicated to all the visionary librarians, past, present and future—children's specialists, archivists, high-tech experts, savvy managers, outspoken advocates, library trustees and public policy wonks. How could anyone write a book without them?

— Lawrence Webster
Pendle Hill, Wallingford, Pennsylvania
April 16, 2012

INDEX

Page numbers in *italics* refer to illustrations.